Ratchet Weeds

A Fictionalized Telling of the Cannabis Tech Industry

Fabian Hernandez

Contents

Chapter 1
A New Day

The sun was just rising in Florida, and the humidity was suffocating. A German sedan pulled into the parking lot of a university's Health Sciences building. It was a small facility in Hollywood, Florida, where late bloomers pursued their lingering dreams of practicing medicine. The driver immediately noticed that there were no other cars in sight. After parking and observing his desolate surroundings, he stepped out of the car and looked through one of the building windows. There were no lights turned on, which confirmed that he was the first person there.

The thirty-year-old graduate student returned to the car to study and continue listening to the national news report. He grabbed a worn-out package of notes that were written in a pattern that only he could understand. To aid his efforts, he reached down to the side-holder of the driver's door and pulled out a glass pipe that was packed with a Sativa strain of cannabis. He took a hit, held the smoke, then exhaled before reclining his car seat and studying comfortably for the next four hours.

The exam ended at noon. The graduate students exited the room. Some looked pleased, and others looked nervous. The early riser, the pothead, felt confident, but he couldn't help to wonder about his response to one particular question. Before walking out of the building in a pensive state of mind, the Dean of the program, Dr. Sathees Patel, approached him.

"Mr. Noah Rodriguez, how are you? How was the exam?"

asked the man from India.

"Dr. Patel, I'm good. The exam went well. I'm glad it's all over. I needed to get a ninety-eight to get an A in the course and boost my average high enough to graduate. I'm hoping I did that."

"Good, I'm sure you did fine. I also wanted to tell you that your letter of recommendation has been mailed," said Dr. Patel.

"Thank you so much, Dr. Patel. I appreciate all your help," replied Noah.

"It's not a problem. Let me know if you need anything else," said Dr. Patel before leaving to talk to other students.

Noah Rodriguez left the building and walked to his car while continuing to ponder the response to that one particular question. He couldn't let it go. He put his bag on the passenger seat and took out his Neuro-anatomy book in hopes of finding the answer in one of the chapters. But his efforts were futile, and he realized that the question came from the professor's personal arsenal.

"Damage to what region of the brain causes a nystagmus?" he asked himself.

Noah drove out of the parking lot while simultaneously running a search for the correct answer on his phone. The car arrived at a traffic light in the hood, and the answer presented itself. It was the Flocculonodular lobe, which was not the answer he picked. Suddenly, Noah found himself at a pivotal crossroads. To him, his mission was clear. There was no room for fear or to let his conscience overwhelm his thought process. He had to retrieve his exam and change the answer without getting caught.

Everything that he'd worked for was at stake. That enormity of significance ignited an impulse to ensure that he was in control of his destiny. Understanding the consequences of his actions, but also the degree of his capabilities, Noah turned the wheel of his car, made an illegal U-turn, and drove back to campus.

He parked his car and walked to the building, determined to somehow change the incorrect answer. Like a stalking wolf, he walked to the administrative assistant's office, where he knew the exams were being held. There, he found Mrs. Robinson talking to a student on the phone. She recognized Noah at the doorway and motioned him to enter and sit on a chair.

"I understand. I know how important this is to you. But the best thing you can do is e-mail Dr. Brown and ask if you can retake the final."

Noah waited for her to finish the conversation. He looked at the desk and noticed the pile of exam folders. It was imperative that he locate his exam as quickly as possible.

"Hi, Noah! How's everything?" asked Mrs. Robinson.

"Hi, Mrs. Robinson. I just took my neuro final, but I think I made a big mistake," said Noah.

"Oh no! What happened?" replied Mrs. Robinson. "I was about to leave when I realized that I may have forgotten to write my name on my exam," said Noah, who'd come to know Mrs. Robinson as the warm, motherly figure of the program.

"Oh, that's not good," said Mrs. Robinson. "You said it was neuro?"

"Yes."

Mrs. Robinson searched through the multiple piles of folders on her desk before locating the one for Neuro- anatomy.

"And here they are," said Mrs. Robinson as she separated the folder. "Just find your answer sheet and make sure your name is there. I wouldn't want you to have to retake the exam."

Noah gladly searched through the pile of exams and found the one with his name.

"Here it is, and yes. I wrote my name. Thanks for letting me check."

"Anytime. I'm glad everything is alright," said Mrs. Robinson.

Noah placed his exam on top of the stack and remembered the location of the folder before leaving the room. Mrs. Robinson walked out with him, and another student pulled her to the side of the hallway.

"Mrs. Robinson, I tried to register online like you said, but the system didn't recognize my student number," said the young Haitian student.

"Okay, this has been happening with a lot of the other students. But let me go talk to Dr. Anderson about a scheduling conflict. As soon as I'm done, I'll come back, and we can register together," said Mrs. Robinson.

She walked down the hallway to Dr. Anderson's office. And that was the opportunity that Noah was looking for. As he stared at her large, curvy ass bounce from side to side, Noah waited to make his move. He made sure that she was engaging in a prolonged conversation with Dr. Anderson before enacting his plan.

She spoke to Dr. Anderson, the Biochemistry professor, who wanted to add a new elective for the next semester. But once Noah saw two other students enter the office and join the conversation with both Mrs. Robinson and the professor, he made his move. He stealthily walked back into her office to alter his test.

Noah opened the folder and immediately located his exam. Fortunately for him, he could still hear Mrs. Robinson talking, so he had some warning as to when she was coming. Fast and focused, he located the question in the test booklet and confirmed the correct response; number twenty-two, choice B, *Flocculonodular lobe.*

"I didn't realize it until it was too late," said Mrs. Robinson to the professor. The conversation had turned casual. "My son was covered in mud from head to toe!"

Noah took out his mechanical pencil, erased the incorrect answer, and replaced it with the correct answer. He blew on the paper to remove any eraser remnants and put it back in the folder. Still in wolf mode, he casually walked out of the room, out of the building, into his car, and drove off the premises.

Noah drove west on Hollywood Boulevard towards I-95 to head south to Miami. He felt as though he'd gotten away with the crime of the century. His adrenaline was pumped, and he was hyped about finishing his graduate program. After getting on the highway, his cell phone rang. He didn't recognize the number with the 954 area-code, but he'd been applying for jobs for the past month and assumed it was a hiring representative. Noah turned down the radio volume and answered the call.

"Hello," he said.

"Hi! Hi! How are you? I'm looking for Noah Rodriguez," said

a stern female voice.

"Yes, this is Noah."

"Hi, Noah. I'm calling you from CannaTron. You submitted a resume for our technical writer position. Um, just a quick question, do you have experience writing RFPs?"

"Um, yes, before graduate school, I was a copywriter at Frankfurt Worldwide Logistics for two years. It was my job to write RFP responses to win shipping bids from large corporations. I also managed the application software manuals, keeping them up-to-date for our end users."

There was a pause in the conversation. Noah could hear the woman talking to someone else as papers rustled in the background. Then another voice joined the conversation. It was a male's voice, sort of.

"Hi, Noah, this is Ian. Um, we're looking for someone to help us write government RFPs. Do you have any experience with that? Writing RFPs for government entities?" said the feminine voice.

"Yes, I wrote multiple RFPs for government contracts while in Frankfurt, as well as commercial RFPs," replied Noah.

Again, there was a pause after his response. Noah could hear the interviewers whispering to each other.

"So, where do you live? Because we're located in Fort Lauderdale," said the female.

"I'm in Miami, right off I-95," he replied while turning onto the express lane.

"Okay, so, here's the thing," said the woman with an indifferent tone. "We're a software company in the cannabis industry. The way it works is every time marijuana is legalized in a state; governments ask businesses to track it with a software program to make sure all of it is accounted for. We are the ones who currently make that software. We need someone to write RFP responses for these state government bids and to also help us with the manuals."

"Our COO is also in need of someone to help him with marketing material, so if you're good with blogs and stuff, that's even better. Does this sound like something you'd be interested in?" asked Ian.

Unknown to the hiring representatives, Noah was at a loss for words. He'd just finished graduate school and immediately got an interview with a marijuana company. He thought it was a perfect fit in every sense of the word. It was simply a coincidence or fate that presented a position with his exact experience.

"Yes, the position sounds interesting. I have no doubt that my work experience can help you with your end goals," said Noah in his most professional tone. He didn't want to give any indication to them that he was actually a "come mierda" stoner.

"So, just to be one hundred percent clear, you are comfortable working in the marijuana industry?" asked the woman.

"Um, yeah, as-long-as it's all legal. I definitely support the legalization movement," replied Noah.

"Well, good. This is definitely a place where you need to feel comfortable to be successful," said the woman.

"Yeah, we all smoke; well, almost everybody. I'm just saying, it's a really cool environment in that sense, but when we need to be professional, we shape up," added Ian.

"You need to fit in, understand?" asked the woman.

"I think we talk the same language. I get it," replied Noah.

"Remember, we work a lot here. I mean, it's normal to work late nights, weekends, whatever it takes," said the stern woman. "Are you willing to work long hours if given the position?"

"Absolutely. I just finished graduate school and am only looking to work," replied Noah.

Again, there was a pause, followed by more whispering.

"Okay, so we're going to send your information to our CEO, Albert Abraham. He's looking to fill the position quickly. So, once he makes a decision, we'll let you know," said the male with a lisp.

"He's been traveling a lot. So, give him at least two days to get back to you," added the woman.

"Alright, no problem, thank you very much. I appreciate you calling me. I'll be waiting for a response," said Noah.

The Miami skyline emerged to the east as he drove on the I-95 overpass through the Golden Glades Interchange. Noah was in disbelief at everything that had happened that day. His mind was racing. So, he picked up his pipe, which still had some weed in it, and took a hit to see if that helped calm his thoughts.

"What a great fucking day!" he said to himself before turning up the radio and cruising down the highway to his home.

Noah arrived at the two-bedroom apartment in Little Havana. He opened the door and was welcomed by his little white mutt, Lola. The dog jumped on the couch, wagging her tail emphatically, and laid on its back to get a belly rub from her master. Noah obliged the scraggly pooch and sat on the couch before expiring a breath of relief for having earned his Master's degree in Biomedical Sciences. A few seconds later, his phone rang. He saw that it was the same number from CannaTron. He wasn't expecting another call so soon, but he answered the phone.

"Hello?" he said.

"Hi, Noah. This is Ian again. Um, Albert saw your samples, and he would like for you to come in for an interview. How does that sound?"

"That sounds excellent. When would you like for me to come in?" asked Noah.

"Um, well, that's the thing. Albert's going out of town tomorrow and won't be back for a week. He really wanted to fill the spot before leaving. Are you available to come in at any time this afternoon?"

Noah was in a rare position, and he knew it. He hadn't worked in over a year and was being supported by his fiancé, Victoria Santana. He needed the job and didn't want to lose the opportunity to another candidate.

"I can come in at three," he said.

"Okay, great. I'll let Albert know. I'm sorry for the rush, but things have been really busy here," said Ian.

"No worries. Thank you again for the opportunity," said Noah.

He hung up the phone and immediately called his fiancé, who was working at a data center hosting company as a marketing coordinator.

"Hello," said Victoria Santana of Atibaia, Brazil.

"Baby! Baby! Guess what?" said Noah.

"Hi, my love. How did your test go?" she asked.

"Good. I'll tell you all about that later. But guess what?"

"What?" she replied.

"I have an interview at a pot company. It's some software company in the marijuana industry, and they need a proposal writer," said an excited Noah.

"Whoa! Cool, baby! Wow! That's good timing," said Victoria.

"I know, right? Okay, just wanted to let you know. I gotta go shave and get dressed. It's in Fort Lauderdale, so I should be getting back when you get home."

"Okay, good luck. I love you," said Victoria. "Oh, hey, I paid the deposit for the DJ today. They said we don't have to pay the rest until one week before the wedding."

"Wow, that's excellent. I love you too," replied Noah. He hung up the phone and got ready for his interview.

Chapter 2
The Interview

The office was situated in the tackiest building of all South Florida. It had a retro-sixties design, almost like something out of a Jetsons cartoon. Noah walked out of the elevator on the sixth floor wearing a black suit and tie. He walked to the double-door and confirmed that it was suite 6-A, as was written in an email that Ian sent. Before knocking, he noticed a stone plaque with a marble frame hanging on the wall. It had a Presidential-like emblem that read [CannaTron: Official Member of the National Marijuana Chamber of Commerce]. To Noah, it looked like something official, something that brought the company notoriety.

To further lure his curiosity, the heavy double-door was locked. He knocked three times to see if anyone would open, but there was no immediate response. After two minutes of waiting, he knocked again, three times. Another minute passed until somebody finally opened the door. She was an older lady in her fifties, a Caucasian with blonde hair and blue eyes, who, he could tell, used to be hot. But now, she looked old and beat, as though she had made many mistakes over the decades.

She welcomed Noah with a bright smile, one that suggested her attraction for him.

"Hello, I'm here for the interview. I spoke with Ian," he said.

"Yes, Hi! I'm Elaine. Please, come in," she said while continuing to stare aggressively at Noah.

She flung her hair and said, "I'm sorry to keep you waiting, but

I was on the phone trying to order the boss' lunch. Uh, I hate dealing with those guys," she said before laughing at her own comment.

She went behind her desk and called somebody to announce Noah's arrival.

"Mr. Rodriguez is here for his interview... very well," she said before hanging up the phone. "It'll just be a minute, hon. Please, take a seat.

"Noah sat in a chair and admired the bright, open room with a panoramic glass wall that overlooked the Intra-coastal waterway. He stared at the water while listening to the classic rock playlist on the secretary's radio. She bopped her head to the beat of the music while pretending to do work. Noah also took notice of the contemporary art on the wall and a framed article about the company. The headline read, LOCAL COMPANY DOMINATING THE POT INDUSTRY.

"Ah, isn't it such a beautiful day?" asked Elaine while looking outside the window, still smiling with her eyes bright and wide.

"Absolutely, and you have nice, relaxing music to enjoy the view," said Noah. "Good tunes."

"Yeah, all I need is a fat joint, and I'm set," said Elaine, catching Noah by surprise. He could only wonder about the company when the secretary openly spoke about pot. *I guess this really is a pot company,* he thought.

A door opened, and another blonde hair, blue-eyed person with an eye-twinkle appeared.

"Hi, Noah. I'm Ian. Thank you for coming on such short

notice," said Ian while faintly shaking Noah's hand and staring him deeply in the eye to get a read on his sexual orientation.

"No problem, thank you for the opportunity," replied Noah in a stern tone.

"Come with me, please," said Ian in his gayest voice possible.

"Good luck, hon," said Elaine.

A horny, old woman and a gay guy; this looks to be interesting, so far, thought Noah.

"Did you find us okay?" asked Ian while escorting Noah to the interview.

"Yeah, I just took the express lane and got off on Broward," said Noah.

"Oh, that sucks. I never have to get on the highway. I live a few minutes away in Wilton Manors."

"Where's that?" asked Noah, who was familiar with most of the tri-county area but had never heard of Wilton Manners.

"It's a few blocks north. It's this little neighborhood," replied Ian.

As they walked through the hallway, Noah felt a serene ambiance in the office. The brief walk was accompanied by more wall-art and meditation music. They arrived at another double-door that was closed. Ian then stopped walking and turned around to address Noah.

"Look, Albert is a little busy right now. So, if he seems a bit rude or wired, don't take it personally. He's actually a really great guy."

"Thanks for the warning," replied Noah.

They entered Albert Abraham's lavish office, which was decorated in French-baroque wooden furniture. The decor also consisted of expensive art and artifacts. Albert was sitting at his desk conducting business through a phone headset while holding a tiny, shaking poodle in his arms. He was overweight, flashy, and wore a cheap toupee and a thousand-dollar Armani suit. At the other end of the room, another blonde hair, blue-eyed woman in a mangled power-suit was sitting on a couch.

"Noah, how are you? Thank you for coming," said Albert as he reached to shake Noah's hand without getting out of his chair.

"This is Brittney. She's Albert's assistant. She was the other person you spoke to on the phone," said Ian about the woman on the couch.

"Executive assistant," affirmed Brittney as she walked over and extended her hand. "You'll be reporting to me," she said while awkwardly smiling and nodding her head. It was a nervous response. Like Elaine, she was also smitten by Noah.

"Please, take a seat," said Albert.

Noah sat down and immediately noticed an electronic smoking pen on Albert's desk. He wondered if the contents in that smoking pen contained weed oil. Ian and Brittney sat on the couch at the other end of the room. They all waited for Albert to finish his call.

"Okay, I understand. I'll watch out for that e-mail, and we'll get together next week for dinner... bye."

Albert hung up the phone and looked around his desk as though he was trying to find something. It wasn't long until he gave up his search. Then he crossed his hands and looked Noah directly in the eyes.

"Noah, I'd like to tell you a bit about the company. We develop software that provides a much-needed solution to the cannabis industry. The software tracks everything from the cultivation, flowering, shipping, and sales of cannabis. Every plant is given a unique barcode number that is used to track it throughout the life cycle. Isn't that nice?" said the well-schooled doctor of psychology, according to his business card, which read Albert Abraham Ph.D.

"Absolutely. I can imagine that you anticipate a lot of business in the upcoming years," said Noah, sounding engaged.

"An immense workload. That's why we need you to help with the RFPs and manuals so that we can have a strong shot at winning those state contracts. I have your samples here. They look good. Can you write manuals like these for us?"

"Yes, it wouldn't be a problem. I managed the technical manuals for Frankfurt Worldwide Logistics for two years," confirmed Noah once again. "I documented an internal shipping application that they created and used to track all shipments."

"Uh huh, uh huh, good... Ian tells me you just finished graduate school. What did you study?" asked Albert. "Biomedical Sciences. I'm looking to get a Ph.D. down the road," replied Noah.

Albert nodded his head while reviewing the work samples that Noah submitted. At the same time, he picked up his electronic pen and took two large puffs. Then he smiled, looked at Noah, and said, "It's wax. Do you want a hit?"

Noah wasn't sure what to say. Of course, he wanted some. But he wasn't sure if he was being tested.

"I mean, if you really want me to...," he said nervously before extending his hand. Albert smiled, pulled back the pen, and laughed hysterically. "It's just tobacco! But I like your guts, kid! You reacted a lot cooler than most people." Albert turned his attention to Ian and continued, "Ian, how much does a writer earn in today's market?"

"It ranges from thirty-six thousand to one hundred thousand," Ian replied.

Albert took a second to think of a figure that he wanted to offer, puckering his lips and looking up at the ceiling.

"I can offer you...sixty thousand a year. How does that sound?" said Albert.

Noah didn't want to lose the position to anyone else. He needed the work and wouldn't leave that place without a job. Additionally, he and Victoria were planning a wedding. Any income would help until he found a higher-paying job. Without hesitation or giving a counteroffer, he accepted the position.

"I'll take it," he replied.

"Excellent! Welcome aboard! Brittney, Ian, do you have anything to add?" said Albert.

Brittney, who looked over-worked, miserable, and like she hadn't had good sex in ages, felt a need to emphasize effort and her seniority at the company.

"I just want to make sure that you understand the hours we'll need. As I said on the phone, we may require overtime, weekends, or whatever. You're a part of my team now. Okay? If I call and say that I need you for something, I really need your full attention."

"I understand. I'm here for whatever you need," replied Noah, who was already getting annoyed with her demeanor. Still, after clearly stating that he understood her requirements, Brittney continued talking down to him.

"Okay, because there are times that we'll need you one hundred percent, no matter the day, okay? Ian slept here for almost a week last month because we had to get two RFPs sent out at the same time, alright? I'm sorry. I'm not trying to turn you away. I just don't want you to come to my office complaining that this wasn't discussed with you."

"It's okay, I understand. I'm on board," replied Noah, who had already concluded that it was going to suck working with her. He also wondered about her education and background. She didn't talk like an educated person. And he wasn't willing to submit to some secretary. To him, that was preposterous.

"Uh, Noah, one more thing. As an employee, here we offer stock options. Everyone out there is dedicated to this company, and it's my intention to make them all rich beyond their wildest dreams. If you work hard and stay loyal, I promise, I'll make you a millionaire when we go public. How does that sound?" said Albert.

"That sounds excellent," said Noah, who didn't believe a word out of his new boss' mouth.

"So, Ian, let's see about getting him some stock," said Albert.

After accepting the position, Ian took Noah on a tour. They first encountered a tall, black gentleman who was blocking the narrow hallway while talking at someone's office doorway. Ian gently put his hand on the man's waist before saying in a sensual manner, "Excuse me, coming through. I got a new one for you."

Noah cringed as the man turned around to get a look at the new meat.

"Helloooo," said the man in a soft tone as Ian and Noah walked towards the communal area.

"That's Eugene Pierre. He's our Chief Technology Officer. I'm sure you'll be working with him a lot," said Ian, making Noah feel a bit uncomfortable with the idea. "Right now, I'm taking you to our HR person, Debbie. We need you to fill out some paperwork and make copies of your identifications. You brought them, right?"

"Yeah, I saw your instructions in the email. I got them right here," replied Noah.

From there, they entered another wing of the office where two pretty ladies were sitting in old cubicles. They were reviewing a sales ledger and chatting at the same time. One was sexy, with long, dark hair and tattoos covering her arms. The other was a dirty-blonde hippie with short, scruffy hair and a hemp neckless around her neck. She was sitting at her desk with her legs crossed on the chair, tucked under an oversized sweater that she wore. They both had weed stickers and pothead marketing material plastered on the ragged walls of their brown cubicles.

"Ladies, this is Noah. He's our new writer. Noah, this is Jamie and Kristin," said Ian.

"Hello, ladies," said Noah with a charming smile.

"Hey!" they replied with pretty smiles and interested eyes.

Ian walked into a large office and said, "And this is Debbie, our HR Manager."

"Yeah, HR, accounting, I do it all," said Debbie sarcastically. She stood up from behind her expensive desk to shake Noah's hand. She was short, heavy-set, and had a bad skin complexion.

"Okay, so I need to go and do something really quick. I'll leave you here with Debbie and come back when you're done with your paperwork," said Ian to Noah.

"Alright, man. Thanks for everything," replied Noah. Noah sat across a large oak desk, thinking that he was in the presence of a prodigy because she was so young but apparently qualified enough to have such a miraculous office. She located and handed Noah a stack of papers to sign while comfortably engaging in personal conversation.

"So, where are you from? I feel that I've seen you before. I dunno, you look very familiar," said Debbie. Noah tried his best to avoid staring at a cystic pimple on her chin, but he couldn't avoid it.

"I'm pretty good at remembering people, and your face doesn't ring a bell. I used to live in Davie while I was at college. Did you go to Nova?"

"Who? Me? No, I didn't finish college. I'm actually taking three courses right now at CC."

What the fuck? Noah thought to himself. *How the fuck are you sitting in this big office, and you're still taking classes at the community college?*

"Oh, that's great. I got my bachelor's at Nova and my Master's degree at Barry. I know how hard it is to balance school and work, but don't worry, you'll pull through." It was Noah's intent to be un-obviously patronizing.

At that moment, a tall, lanky character with a slicked 1950's haircut approached Debbie's doorway. He curiously walked into the room and extended his hand to Noah, who was sitting in the chair.

"Hi, I'm David Yanowitz. Welcome to the team. Are you a local?" asked David in his soft tone.

That was when Noah realized that he would be working in a gay-dominated environment. His homophobia was innocent but existent. He wasn't uncomfortable with the idea of working with gay people. But his conservative and overly masculine upbringing rarely exposed him to that culture. So, he didn't know what to expect.

"Hi, David. I live in Miami with my fiancé. But I've lived in South Florida all my life," he said in his manliest voice.

"Oh, nice. A lot of us here live in Wilton Manors. I was just wondering if you were one of our neighbors. Well, welcome," said David. "Uh, Debbie. I'm so dumb. I forgot what I came to ask you. I'll come back when I remember. It was nice meeting you, Noah."

"Likewise," replied Noah.

His mind still couldn't wrap itself around the fact that Debbie was the HR Manager of the company. Her lack of education, a finance degree, or a CPA license made him seriously question the validity of the company. And it wasn't easy for him to keep his mouth shut about the matter.

"Are you really the HR Manager and the accountant for the company?" asked Noah.

"That's right. I mean, I'm not really an accountant, but I look over Albert's financial statements. I also overlook the hiring process and do a little administrative work. I've even taken Albert's car to the carwash before."

"Is that on your job description, too?" asked Noah.

"No, but at some point, I think everyone here has taken Albert's car to get a wash. So, don't be surprised if you get asked one day," replied Debbie.

Yeah fucking right, thought Noah.

After finishing the paperwork, Ian returned to escort Noah out of the building. But there were still two other employees for Noah to meet. The first was an early-thirties white male in a suit who projected a confident demeanor.

"Zack Stansbury, this is our new writer, Noah Rodriguez," said Ian. "Noah, this is Zack Stansbury, our Investment Director.

Zack stood up and walked around his desk, back straight and shoulders squared. He looked Noah in the eyes and gave him a firm handshake. *Finally, a straight fella,* thought Noah.

"Noah, good to meet you. Welcome, I'm Zack," he said in a raspy, surfer tone.

"It's good to meet you, Zack," replied Noah.

"So, you're going to write RFPs? God, good luck with that. I remember writing a few of those," said Zack.

"I'm sure I'll be alright," replied Noah.

"Hey, anything you need, let me know. I actually have a meeting with Albert right now. He doesn't like it when his money arrives late," said Zack. He looked at Ian, adjusted his suit, and said before walking away, "Ian, always a pleasure."

While walking toward the exit, Ian took Noah to meet one last person. They walked through the glass doors of a conference room where a small, thin, Asian man was typing away on a laptop. He was heavily focused on his work and looked exhausted beyond description. He could barely open his eyes.

"Hey, Kenny! This is Noah, our new RFP writer. Noah, Kenny Cho is the one who currently writes our RFPs. But he's just been promoted to Co-CEO and doesn't have time to write anymore."

Kenny Cho, who was dressed in a hood, jeans, and sneakers, shook Noah's hand. He took a deep breath to gather his thoughts and then spoke in an articulate manner.

"Welcome to the team. It's good to have you on board. Let me know if there's anything you need. Sorry I can't talk any longer, but I need to finish this presentation."

"No worries, I understand," said Noah, who got the impression that Kenny was somewhat rude and arrogant. "I'm looking forward to working with you."

Kenny returned to his immense workload while Noah and Ian left the room. They arrived at the front doors of the office, and before exiting, Noah asked, "Hey, Ian, I was wondering. Are we allowed to smoke pot in the office? I couldn't help but notice a fruity smell in the air."

"First off, we're really trying to stick to the word 'cannabis' instead of weed or pot. So remember that when you're writing. As to your question, no, we don't allow any cannabis on the premises. It's illegal. But don't worry, everyone here smokes, just on their own time," replied Ian with a bright smile. "That smell might be from the vape pens. We do have a few people in the office who smoke those."

Back at the apartment, Victoria was busy creating social media posts for her job. Noah opened the door and was welcomed by Lola. As always, her tail was wagging, and she was looking for a few kisses and a belly rub.

"Hi, baby. Here, sit, smoke, and tell me about the new job," said Victoria while handing him a fresh bowl that she had packed.

Noah, still energized from the events of the day, sat on the edge of the couch, took the bowl, and took a rip.

"There's just so much to tell you," he said before taking a hit. "But first, let me tell you about this place. It's for a proposal writer position which pays sixty thousand. The job seems cool. The pay kinda sucks, and the place gave me this weird vibe. I mean, I don't have a problem with gay people, but there were too many homos in one place at one time. I mean, why is everyone gay at that place? Why would they want to hire me? I mean, I walked in with a suit and tie, no flashy colors, very conservative."

Victoria just rolled her eyes. Unlike her paranoid fiancé, her mind wasn't filled with such nonsense.

"I highly doubt anybody is going to try and fuck you. Gay people aren't normally like that. Everybody has a type. So, I think you'll be fine. Was everyone nice?"

"Yeah, everyone was nice. There was just something shady in the air. The owner of the company looked like a corrupt, mafiosotype. He offered me a vape hit, pretending like it was pot, to see how I'd react. And he sits there while holding a little, shaky poodle."

"What did you do when he offered you a hit?" asked Victoria.

"I reached for it with confidence," replied Noah.

"But it's the pot industry? What do they do? Is it all legal?" asked Victoria, who over-analyzed most scenarios.

"These guys bid for government contracts. They make software that tracks the pot throughout the supply chain and reports the numbers to the state government and law enforcement. Apparently, it's a unique solution to the industry."

Noah and Victoria discussed the details of the day over a few bowls of fresh green. To them, things like school, a good job, and good weed mattered. It wasn't a normal relationship by any means because it was too normal. They both worked, studied, smoked, exercised, and made love on a routine basis. They supported each other's goals and visualized a prosperous future together.

Chapter 3
The First Day

Noah left his apartment early on that first day and arrived at the parking lot a half hour before the start time. After looking at himself in the mirror and taking a deep breath, he stepped out of the car and walked to the front of the building. There, he found Brittney smoking a morning cigarette with another gentleman.

"Hi, Noah! Ready for your first day?" said Brittney, who had an outdated, early-nineties blowout hairstyle. She took a drag of her cigarette and blew out the smoke while aggressively admiring Noah's physique.

"I am," he replied.

"Good, you better be," she rudely replied. "Oh, Noah, I would like for you to meet our COO, Aziz Bashir. He was out of town the day you interviewed."

Noah extended his hand to greet his new boss. Aziz took notice and briefly froze. Then he put the cigarette in his mouth before shaking hands. It was like he wasn't used to dealing with any sort of professionalism.

"Hi, Noah; good to meet you, Aziz. I'm glad to have you on board. I have some marketing content that I'd like to review with you and get your content expertise opinion," said Aziz.

That's one shady-ass, weasel-looking motherfucker, if I've ever seen one, was Noah's initial thought of Aziz, who also looked high as a kite.

"I'm looking forward to working with you," he replied. Like everyone on the planet, he was two-faced to some degree. But to survive in corporate America, he had to learn to hide his true feelings all the time.

Ian was waiting outside the office when Noah got out of the elevator. He greeted Noah with his bright smile and sparkling eyes before saying, "Missster Rodriguez!" To Noah, Ian was a perfect example of the fact that being gay wasn't a choice. He knew CannaTron would be different, unlike anywhere else he'd ever worked. Whatever was waiting for him in that office, he knew that it was going to be something authentic, something that would rattle his core beliefs.

They entered the office, and Elaine was at the front desk, smiling as always.

"Hi-ya, hon! Welcome back!" she said.

Ian took Noah through the second door and down the hall to his new work area. Along the way, Noah could hear yelling coming from Albert's office. It sounded like he wasn't happy with somebody's work performance. It sounded like that person was about to get fired.

"So, right now, we're kind of low on offices. I think there is one freeing up which we will give to you. But until then, you can use this office. It normally belongs to our Director of Government Relations, Robert Peterson, but he had surgery and will be out for the next few weeks," said Ian.

Noah looked around the spacious office and felt a degree of respect. The fact that he was being offered an office spoke volumes about the company's commitment to recruiting talent such as himself. Then he thought of Debbie and remembered that, up to that point, she had set the bar.

"So, take a seat, settle in, and Zack Stansbury should be here shortly to give you a training session on the software. For now, just review these RFPs." The binders were massive. "I have the one for California and for Colorado. These aren't winners, but they're all the same. Well, almost the same. And here are your username and password for your email. Just open the browser on your desktop and enter these credentials," continued Ian. He wrote the credentials on a post-it and left it hanging on Noah's desk.

"Thanks, Ian! Thanks for everything," said Noah before Ian left the room.

Despite the sense of awkwardness that he felt about the company, it was clear to Noah that work was being accomplished at CannaTron. The RFP was thorough with information about the product and the company's operations. It contained technical screenshots, a statement of work, a financial summary of operating costs, a sales plan, and a summary of the executive team. As he was reading with interest, his email inbox chimed. It was a mail from Aziz that read:

Noah, can you please review the brochures and flyers for me? I'll come by later with Mitch Walsh to hear your ideas. We'd like to take this entire thing to another level and really make ourselves stand apart at the shows.

Aziz

Noah opened and reviewed the document attachments. As he was reading about CannaTron's "Industry Commitment" philosophy, he noticed the salesgirl with the tattoos, Jamie, linger back and forth by the office door. On the surface, she made it look as though she needed to speak to Brittney about something. But it was obvious to him that she was also trying to get his attention. He was all too familiar with the perks of being the new guy.

"Hey, have you seen Brittney?" she turned and said to him. She stood in a selfie-pose that accentuated her finest features, especially her perfect breasts.

"Yes, she was downstairs having a cigarette," said Noah. She rolled her eyes and said, "Oh, okay, thanks. How's your first day going?"

"Good, so far. Thanks for asking," replied Noah with a charming smile.

"Well, don't hold your breath on that," she said with a smile before walking away.

Ten minutes later, Zack Stansbury entered the office wearing a suit, no tie, and holding a computer. His eyes were glassy. His face was flushed. Noah could smell the alcohol seeping from his pores.

"Noah, what's up!?" said Zack before sitting down and taking a deep breath to try to gain some type of composure. His head was spinning after another long night at the strip club. "So, we were supposed to start this training in ten minutes, but we have to wait a little longer for Bryan Miller. He's another new hire who is still on his way."

"No problem. Are you doing alright? It looks like they've been working you hard," said Noah. He respected Zack for trying to work through the hangover.

"You have no idea, bro," said Zack as he yawned. Then he shook his head, looked at Noah, and laughed. "Alright, I, uh, gotta go back to my office." Zack slapped his knees with both hands and stood out of the chair. "See you in an hour in the conference room," he said before leaving the room.

As he scrolled through the plethora of documentation and content, it didn't take long for Noah to realize how reliant everybody was on Brittney. For the next hour, he saw person after person walk into her office for one thing or another. Noah could hear the stress weigh down on her every time someone vented a request or a complaint.

"Brittney! Can you approve this? I can't find Aziz anywhere," said Jamie while rushing into her office. Again, Brittney was out having another cigarette when Jamie arrived. "Uh, she's never fucking here when I need her," blurted Jamie while walking back to her cubicle.

"Brittney! Where the fuck is blondie?" said a large, older woman with a short, boyish haircut. After looking in the office and not seeing Brittney, she said, "This is bullshit. I don't know how we get anything done here. Fuck these assholes."

Ten minutes later, Brittney returned to her office after the third cigarette of the day. She found Ian standing at the door, impatient and with his arms crossed. "Hey, I've booked three interviews today. Are you going sit in with me?"

"Ian, I really don't know. I mean, we have these investors coming tomorrow to meet Albert. I still need to book flights for Kenny and AJ," said Brittney while sitting at her desk, holding up her head with her arm. "What time do they start?"

"At two," replied Ian. "You're the one who told me to make the job posting. If you're going to be working with these people, I think you need to be there."

"You know, Ian, sometimes I just wish people here could handle their own shit. Uh, I'm going down for another smoke," said Brittney before storming out of the office. Noah heard the front door slam, and he laughed. At that moment, Ian walked by the office and rolled his eyes.

"Welcome to CannaTron," he said sarcastically to Noah while walking away.

As Ian left, he noticed another gentleman walk through the area. He was as colorful of a character as one can expect to see on any normal day. He wore eye liner, eccentric piercings, a choker necklace, a purple and pink t-shirt, and tight, checkered pants. His nails were painted black, and his glowing blonde hair was combed to one side. His style wasn't punk rock or emo. It was something else, something from another dimension. He was handling an assignment for Albert and had been walking frantically through the hallway all morning.

"Lawrence, this isn't what I asked for. I really need you to pay closer attention to my instructions," scolded Albert.

"Albert, I'm really trying. I thought this was everything you wanted to see," replied soft-spoken Lawrence. That was when Noah realized that Lawrence was the person who had been scolded by Albert all day.

Two hours later, Noah was sitting in a conference room with the other new employee, Bryan Miller, who was casually eating an apple. He looked to be near the same age as Noah, a short, stocky guy with a buzzed haircut. The two waited quietly for five minutes without speaking to each other until Noah broke the ice.

"You think this guy's coming?" he asked Bryan.

"Not sure, I saw him an hour ago, but he looked a little...," said Bryan before insinuating that Zack was drunk by chugging drinks in the air with his hand.

After his apple was done, Bryan nonchalantly took hits from an oil pen to pass the time. Noah took notice and couldn't believe his eyes. This guy is smoking weed, he thought. Suddenly, there was an urge to ask for a hit, but he hesitated. They sat and waited for another ten minutes until Zack finally arrived. He walked tall through the glass doors trying to project professionalism, but Noah and Bryan knew better. They looked at each other and chuckled.

Zack attempted to set up his computer to the projector but was unable to get the feed on the large screen. Due to the hangover, his patience was non-existent, and he quickly became frustrated with the situation. He felt sleepy, nauseous, and had a massive headache; he was in no position to operate technology. He clicked and tapped aggressively on his computer as Noah and Bryan watched the shit-show that unfolded.

"What the fuck? I swear to God, nothing works in this place," he grumbled to himself while crouching to insert the HDMI cable into a television input.

After trying three different HDMI ports, Zack gave up. He stood with his face beet-red. He didn't have the patience to call and wait for the IT manager because his hangover was feeling worse by the second. But Zack knew that he had to deliver a demo because he wanted to prove to Kenny that he could present the software to customers. That was the role that many workers at CannaTron sought because it came with traveling privileges. It didn't matter what position a person was hired for. They all wanted to give demos. The problem was that hardly any of them were smart enough to fully understand the technology.

"Alright, guys, I'm just going to wing it on my computer. I guess we can all sit closer together while I take you through the program," said Zack in a hoarse voice. "Gather around."

He sat between Noah and Bryan and attempted to open the program on his computer, but an error prompt displayed on the desktop. Zack sighed and said, "I swear to God, this is bullshit. I'm sorry, guys. This was all supposed to be fixed by today. I don't even think this thing is picking up the Wi-Fi signal."

Bryan Miller could no longer contain his true nature after that. He'd remained quiet for too long, especially while witnessing Zack's bullshit efforts. Perhaps it was because he felt comfortable with two other men who, likely, were pot heads and were straight, but he burst out the most sarcastic laugh imaginable.

"Bbbbbbbffffffffffffff...," he sounded with his mouth puffed, his eyes wide, and a confused smirk across his face. He couldn't contain his opinion about the stupidity of the matter.

Noah laughed at Bryan's comedic antics before telling Zack, "It's alright, man. I mean, you don't look so hot. I have no problem if you want to reschedule."

"Really? I don't look good?" asked Zack.

"Not really," replied Noah.

"Drink much?" said Bryan.

"Only about ten scotches last night! But the pussy was worth it," said Zack before opening his eyes and sticking out his tongue, sending the others into a laughing frenzy.

"Ohhhhh!" expressed Noah.

"Yeah, but was the AIDS?" said Bryan.

"Ohhhhh!" expressed Zack even louder.

"Hey, Zack, this is what they love," said Bryan as he flexed both of his arms like a dumb jock. The testosterone level in the room was at full capacity.

After receiving a second computer prompt denying access to the system, Zack closed the laptop. He had no choice but to abandon the demo presentation. Bryan, leaning back in his chair with his legs crossed, took another hit of his pen. Noah could no longer refrain from asking what was on his mind.

"Is that weed oil?"

"No, it's CBD," replied Bryan.

"Ah, yes. The uh, medicine part. I've only heard about it on those Gupta specials about medical pot. Do you feel anything?" asked Noah.

"Not euphoria, but I do feel well. My breathing is good, and I'm not tired. I just feel well. There is a ton of research out there that says it helps with regulating blood pressure, MS, Chron's disease, and insomnia. I'll email you some reading material that'll catch you up."

"Alright, fuck this. We're just going to have to reschedule," said Zack after running his hands through his face.

After the botched demo session, Noah went back to his temporary office to eat lunch. He continued to review the old RFP responses, becoming impressed with Albert Abraham and AJ Lauria, the programmer who wrote the software code. Together, they found a niche and delivered a solution. Noah had yet to meet AJ, but he imagined him to be a genius.

While finishing his review of the Colorado RFP, Noah heard Elaine being scolded by Brittney. It was an uncomfortable encounter for any new employee to witness. He could feel the abuse and assumed that it wasn't the first time it had happened. Poor Elaine had no choice but to take it.

"Do you even want to work here? I mean, how hard is it for you to do your job? You really have to be pretty stupid to mess this up," said Brittney.

"I'm sorry, I thought you said...," replied Elaine before being rudely interrupted.

"That's always the problem with you, Elaine. I thought, I thought, I thought. Stop thinking and do what I say," said Brittney before walking away, leaving Elaine in tears.

The thrashing occurred within the customer support room in front of the ten-member team. They were the lowest-paid employees of the company, making about thirteen dollars an hour without benefits. Their work area was situated in the center of the office, where no natural light entered, making it a cold and dreary place. Since the area was across from Brittney's office, they were the ones who witnessed her abuse the most, making them all resentful towards her.

Noah was putting away his lunch Tupperware when Aziz

walked into the room with a tall gentleman. From an ethnic perspective, he was as white as white could be, with a cheap haircut, brown hair, and deep blue eyes.

"Noah, this is Mitch. He works in marketing," said Aziz. Noah and Mitch shook hands as the COO started to discuss their needs. "So, we want to review this marketing content with you. Currently, we use these flyers." He handed Noah the outdated flyers. "But we really need to develop stronger content and redo these things. Mitch here attends our trade shows. He has a bit more insight into what's needed."

Noah reviewed the marketing pieces as Mitch started to talk. The brochures were cheap and lacked inspiration. In his opinion, he was looking at something that was expected from someone with no relevant work experience. The grammar was erroneous, the document had no structure, and the images looked like nineties clip art.

"I'm really glad you're here. We've needed a writer on the team for a long time. This stuff that we use is completely outdated. Now, my vision is to consolidate these five pieces into one piece."

Mitch Walsh showed Noah the marketing pieces for the principal features of the management software. The features addressed the stages of cannabis production; cultivation, processing, and retail sales.

"I feel that potential customers don't get it. We need to take these individual pieces and somehow explain them to the customers in a way that's less confusing."

"Sounds like we should create a single document with separate sections or chapters that thoroughly explain these bullet points," said Noah.

"Exactly, thank you! That's what I've been trying to explain that we need this entire time. While I'm at the shows, I want to hand these things out to everyone who walks in front of me and leave them without any choice other than us," said Mitch.

"Do you have an example of what our competitors use?" asked Noah.

"No, not really; our only competitors are E-Greens and Cyber Track, but they're way behind us in every regard. Their software fails, and customers are unhappy all the time. We need to put them in their place and show them that they can't compete with us. With strong writing material, we'll step on their throats and crush their windpipes," said Mitch with fierceness in his voice.

"Damn, Mitch, calm down. You're going to scare Noah away," humorously said Aziz.

"Don't worry about me. I like his enthusiasm," replied Noah, who actually thought that Mitch sounded ridiculous.

"That's why I knew you were a good fit. You look like a tough guy. We need tough guys, no pussies. It's our job to destroy the competition. We need something amazing for the Nevada show that's going to get the job done. They've legalized and are expected to release an RFP soon. I can't emphasize enough that we really need to look strong at the show," said Mitch.

The entire time that Mitch blabbed about his marketing vision, Noah couldn't stop convincing himself that Mr. Aziz Bashir was some type of gangster. From his slick hair to his stoned face and poor complexion, the business clothing that was two sizes too large for him, and the five-thousand-dollar Rolex watch, Noah knew that

Mr. Bashir was up to something illegal. His street- smarts could sense it.

Based on Mitch's further explanation, trade shows were everything in the pot industry. It was the strongest way to market to customers, investors, and entrepreneurs looking to exploit the market's earning potential. The conventions were held all over the country, especially in the Pacific Northwest, Colorado, and states where legalization was being sought. Most business hopefuls had little idea of what they were doing because little was known about state regulations or government compliance. Cannatron's leaders were compliance specialists, which they often emphasized as a selling point.

The rest of the afternoon was quiet after the meeting with Aziz and Mitch. Noah was gathering his belongings to go home when Brittney walked into the office in her heels and short skirt. She had a look of concern on her face as though she was already expecting Noah to quit or have a complaint.

"Hey, how's it going? What are you up to?" she asked.

"I've just been reviewing the RFPs, getting familiar with the program, and now getting ready to go home," replied Noah.

"Good, so, you had a good day?" she asked.

"Yeah, it was fine. Everyone was nice. I also noticed how busy you are," said Noah.

"Do you see that?" She sighed. "People need to really learn how to do their own work. I really don't want to be mean. But as Albert's assistant, I already have enough on my plate. You know?" said Brittney.

"Yeah, it's the only way things get done. They can't expect you to babysit all the time," replied Noah, who thought she was kind of a bitch.

She closed the door and sat in the chair across from Noah. She spread her legs just enough to give him a peak of her red thong. To cover the fact, she started talking about the importance of them having a strong, working relationship. Noah certainly took notice of her actions. He tried not to be so obvious, but it was impossible not to stare.

"Hey, look. I know I come off strong sometimes, as I did in the interview. But as you can see, I've got too much to deal with. I just really need to make sure that you're on board. We brought you in because we feel that you can be a real asset to the proposal team. Like I said before when these RFPs come in, everything else that you do is dropped. We go into full RFP mode, ok?" said Brittney. "You and I are going to spend a lot of time together writing these damned things. I mean, do you have a girlfriend, wife, or fiancé?"

"Yeah, I live with my fiancé," replied Noah, who could only think of one reason why she would ask that. He could sense her interest.

"Well, I really hope she doesn't have a problem with you and me working together. I'm talking nights, days, weekends," said Brittney. "Whatever it takes."

This chick totally wants to fuck, thought Noah. On the surface, he made it seem like he didn't have a clue. But Noah knew every time a woman was hitting on him. It was an instinct that developed cognitively through the years.

"As I said, Brittney, I'm all in. Whatever you need, whatever is needed, I'll be here," replied Noah to let her know that the opportunity was possibly there.

"Well, great. Other than that, I just want to say welcome again, and I'm looking forward to working with you," she said. All the while, the unspoken connection lingered in the air.

"Thanks, Brittney. Me too," replied Noah.

"Well, good," replied Brittney. She stood up, opened the door, and started walking out of the room. But before leaving, she remembered one last thing to say. "Oh Yeah, we have some investors coming tomorrow, so wear a suit. That's another thing. We got a lot of potential investors who come here, government guys too. We don't want to be like those other cannabis companies. Got it?"

"No problem, understood," said Noah.

She left the room, and he exhaled a deep breath. The day was an educating experience, and he could only wonder about the hogwash that awaited.

Chapter 4
The Setback

The first month at Canna Tron was slow for Noah. There were no RFPs released, although the Washington State Liquor and Cannabis Board were expected to release one at any time. Therefore, Noah had plenty of time to observe the company and learn about the cannabis industry. It didn't take long for him to conclude that neither the company nor the cannabis industry was structured to a capacity that demanded respect. The entire industry was still in its infancy.

CannaTron's workforce consisted of a collection of misfits that Albert hired, for cheap, to sell and support the software application that he created with AJ Lauria. At the time that Noah was hired, the company was allocating the earnings it received from winning the New York and Oregon state contracts. They were looking to upgrade the level of workers in the hope of building credibility and fixing the inadequacies of the business model.

At the time, the company's strategy primarily focused on understanding federal legislature and selling the product to retailers through direct sales calls. They had a handful of employees on the ground giving demos to government organizations and high-end customers. These customers included marijuana grows, laboratory facilities, and retail dispensaries.

Regardless of how poorly the company was being managed, Noah finished his first assignment within the month. The final marketing piece was a technical package that thoroughly introduced the company and discussed key points of the software.

It was a far improvement from the one-paged laminate that was previously being distributed. After the final edit, he emailed a copy to Aziz, Mitch, Brittney, and Kenny. Immediately after, he walked to Mitch's cubicle to review the piece with him. But to his surprise, Mitch showed little interest.

"Hey, man, I just sent you the final copy of the marketing package. Check it out and let me know if it's alright," said Noah.

"Sure, I'll review it this afternoon," he said in a mono- tone demeanor while staring closely at his computer. Noah noticed that he was struggling to format a typed document on Word. "I'll probably stay here with Brittney tonight to print these things before I fly out to the show tomorrow, but thanks," said Mitch.

Noah went back to his temporary desk and saw an email from Aziz that read:

This is excellent. It proves that you are a capable and autonomous worker. Something that we really need. Good job.

Aziz

The email was cc'd to the entire company. Some of the employees replied by saying, 'Good job!' or 'Awesome!' Even Albert demonstrated his appreciation:

Thank you for your efforts. It's clear that I made a wise decision by hiring you.

Albert

Other people, like Kenny and Mitch, didn't reply at all. Still, Noah finished that day on a high note. He felt good for being commended for his work and started to see CannaTron as a place where he could be a massive fish in a small pond. There was an opportunity to seize while his future was unknown, and he was an opportunist on the lookout for his own interests.

He arrived early to work the next day to see the final publication before Mitch left for Nevada. He walked directly to Brittney's office, and, as always, she looked exhausted and miserable. By that point, Noah accepted that her bitchiness and poor attitude were a daily thing to endure. She'd yet to be disrespectful to him, but he couldn't ignore the way she treated other people and the way they feared her. He despised seeing that.

"Hey, do you have a copy of the marketing piece for Nevada?"

"Um, yeah, they're right over there on the bookshelf. They came out really nice," said Brittney.

The piece was given a cover sheet that was designed by the on-site graphic designer, making a final product that was visually and informatively appealing. At least, that's what it was supposed to be until Noah opened it and realized that Mitch didn't use his content.

"Um, what the fuck is this?" said Noah while skimming the package.

"What do you mean? What's wrong?" replied Brittney.

"This isn't the content I wrote. None of it is. This looks like a lot of the same stuff that was being used, none of my content. I mean, the grammar is awful. I see two run-ons and three missing commas on the first page alone."

"Are you serious? Why isn't your content there?" asked Brittney. "I used what you sent to Mitch, and he sent to me. Is that not it?"

"No, it's not what I sent Mitch. I guess he decided at the last minute to use his content instead," said Noah.

"He's not supposed to do that. You're the writer. This is why we hired you. I can't believe this. Now, I have to go back to the print shop and print and bind another fifty of these things within the next hour," replied Brittney.

"I mean, is Mitch a boss or something? Because I'm pretty upset that he did this behind my back without any notification. I worked hard on that thing," said Noah while continuing to stand and review the entire piece.

"Who? Mitch? No, he is not a boss, not by a long shot. He's just a sales guy. That's it. It didn't go so well for him in sales, so he asked Aziz to put him in a marketing role," replied Brittney. "He's just transitioning now. We don't even know if this will work out."

"Ah, so he's the jealous type. He didn't want me to overshadow him. Alright, I see it," said Noah, who was trying his best to hide the rage he felt.

"Look, I'm letting you know, be careful with some of these guys. There are a lot of people trying to claw their way into Albert's pocket because some executive changes have been made recently. Okay? Don't let anybody try to push their work off to you, either. 'Cause I know there are a few people who like to do that here," explained Brittney.

"Well, thanks for the heads-up," said Noah, who was a bit in disbelief at the entire situation. *How can any of this be allowed to happen? What kind of a fucking place is this?* He thought to himself.

"It's true. The only people you answer to are Albert, Kenny, Aziz, and me, sort of. Other than that, let me know if there are people trying to hand off work to you or get credit for your work. Now that everyone knows you're a good writer, the vultures will try to take advantage or keep you down."

"What do you mean by that?" asked Noah.

"I just know that there are people here who may not be as good a writer as you and are looking for an opportunity to hand off their work."

Noah took a minute to wrap his brain around everything he was hearing. He couldn't believe that such behavior was knowingly happening and being tolerated. It was an eye-opening experience knowing that he couldn't trust his co-workers.

"So, what are we going to do about this Mitch ordeal?" asked Noah.

"I'm going to talk to him, and I'll inform Aziz and Kenny. Then I'll send Ian to the print shop to redo these things. I just need you to send me a copy of the document. Does it have the cover sheet and everything?" asked Brittney.

"Yeah, I have the final piece. I'll send it to you right now," replied Noah.

"Okay? Is everything alright now?" asked Brittney to try and further diffuse the situation.

"Yeah, I'm good, I guess," said Noah with an unconvincing tone.

"Okay, good. By the way, you're looking really good today. Hell, you always look good. I might have to take you away from that girlfriend of yours," said Brittney.

Noah couldn't believe how direct she was. He sensed something wrong with the entirety of the situation, although he was flattered.

"Oh, so this is really going to happen?" said Noah jokingly.

"Yep, I think it is," replied Brittney, who wasn't joking. "You're so hot; now get the fuck out of my office."

As committed as he'd been to Victoria for almost five years, it made him feel good that another woman desired him with such passion. It let him know that he still had "it." He turned around and walked out of the office, leaving Brittney horny and wet. She exhaled a deep breath after the door closed.

Noah waited in his temporary office that morning until Mitch arrived at work. His instinct was to be confrontational and challenge Mitch's manhood by insulting him, hoping it would lead to a fight. But he didn't want to get fired and knew that he had to maintain his composure. Regardless, he knew that he had to say something. Otherwise, the other employees would think he was soft. That mattered a lot to a prideful man like Noah. The second he heard Mitch's voice in the communal area, he stood from his chair to confront the issue.

"Hey, I don't know why the fuck you decided to remove my content from the marketing piece. That shit you added is garbage and makes this company look stupid." In the end, Noah opted for the confrontational approach.

"Look, I just thought it could use some tweaks. I didn't mean to step over the boundaries. I just wanted to give you more time to learn the product before having to handle this type of assignment," explained Mitch, who sounded as though he anticipated backlash for his actions. Brittney heard the commotion and stepped in to hear Mitch's explanation.

"You should have told somebody that you were going to do this. From my understanding, Aziz and Albert approved Noah's version, and it didn't need to be changed. Now I have Ian reprinting these things at the last minute, doubling our marketing costs for the project. You're lucky that Noah brought it to my attention before it was too late. Otherwise, Abraham would've looked like a fool, and you would have been gone. Remember, I'm only saying this once. Mitch, you're not the writer. Noah is. He doesn't answer to you. Got it?"

"Yeah, yeah, whatever," replied Mitch before rudely turning around to walk away.

"Are we going to have a problem, Mitch?" sternly asked Brittney.

"No," replied Mitch.

"What? I didn't hear you?" said Brittney to test her seniority.

"No! Okay!? I got it," said Mitch after turning around to address Brittney.

"You're lucky that you're leaving tomorrow. Otherwise, you'd be washing Albert's car during your lunch break. Or mine!" said Brittney.

There was nothing that Mitch could do. For one, he did wrong, and he knew it. For two, he loved that company and the industry too much to let Brittney take it away from him. He rolled his eyes and walked back to his cubicle. Brittney looked at Noah and nodded her head as though she was saying, 'that's right, I'm the boss.'

At the show, all in the past was forgotten. Mitch stood side-by-side with Albert, Kenny, and Aziz, who all handed out the marketing material with pride. In a world where hardly anybody cared about their personal appearance, Canna Tron looked trustworthy and reliable among the business hippies. More importantly, they sent a strong message to state officials of their worthiness for the cannabis tracking contract.

Noah returned to work the following Monday to find another encouraging email from Albert in his inbox. It was sent out to the entire company, detailing their success at the event. He finished the email by personally thanking Noah for *"creating something that we never had at this company."*

After reading the email, a content Noah went to the kitchen to grab a cup of coffee. There, he ran into Bryan Miller, who was heating up a sandwich in the toaster oven. The two hadn't spoken much up until that point. But Bryan was easily approachable due to his lite nature. Noah also found him to be hilarious.

"Whoa! There he is, Mr. Big Shot!" said Bryan. "Good job on the marketing thing, bro."

"Thanks, man. To be honest with you, it wasn't anything special. But I'm glad I could help. So, what's up with you? What have you been working on?" asked Noah.

Bryan took a deep breath to vent his frustration and said, "Not much. It's been slow. I'm just getting familiar with the Illinois compliance requirements, but that's all."

"What position were you hired for?" asked Noah.

"As a junior associate to Jerry, the company lawyer," replied Bryan.

"You're a lawyer?" asked Noah.

"Yes and no; I have a law degree, but I haven't passed the Bar exam," admitted Bryan.

"How many times have you taken it?" asked Noah.

"This will be my third time," replied Bryan.

Noah could relate to Bryan's situation. Their proximity in age, their immature humor, and their achieved level of education neither was near the top of his graduating class nor where he wanted to be in life. But like Bryan, Noah was a survivor, determined, someone who wasn't given much of a chance to succeed in life but surpassed expectations. They were both bright, intuitive, and fearless.

"So, what are you doing until then?" asked Noah while pouring himself a cup of coffee.

"I was told that I'll be working with Robert Peterson and the government team. But I think Kenny will confirm that when he comes back from Vegas," said Bryan while adding mayonnaise to his gourmet sandwich."

"Damn, dude. I don't want your food, but that's a nice sandwich. Did you pick it up at a restaurant this morning?"

"Nope. These are from my mom. She makes them for me."

"You live with your mom?" asked Noah.

"Yeah, I just moved from St. Augustine. My wife is still there, but as soon as I got this job, I had to move. This is where I want to be."

"So, you guys are just figuring out the next step?"

"Pretty much. She's been with her company for six years, and I still have to save money while I'm here. Hopefully, I can bring her down within a year," revealed Bryan.

"Good luck, man. I'm engaged. I live with my fiancé in Miami, but we're looking to move either here or to Palm Beach County. We're just tired of Miami and need something new."

"Did you go to school?"

"Yeah, I have a Master's degree in bio-sciences from Barry University." Noah didn't feel he was lying because he had taken all the core courses.

"Whoa, that's crazy. I went to Barry Law School. What do you want to be, a doctor?" asked Bryan while taking a bite out of his sandwich.

"Something like that. But I'm still figuring it out."

"Well, man, sounds like you're on a good track. As far as this place, if you want to be in the marijuana industry, you're in the right spot. Trust me; everyone is going gaga over the system. But I gotta get back to my office. Good talk," said Bryan while throwing away his paper plate and wiping tomato and mayonnaise from his face.

Noah went back to his temporary office and saw a gentleman standing at the doorway. He was an older man in his early sixties with a thick, white mustache to cover his beat-red face. Noah thought the man looked like he was on the brink of a heart attack.

"Hi, excuse me. I think I'm in your office," said Noah.

"Yeah, hi, I'm Robert, Director of Government Relations. And you are?"

"I'm Noah Rodriguez. I'm the RFP writer. I've been here for a month because my office situation is still being arranged."

"Yeah, I was recovering from surgery. I heard that we hired you."

As Noah was grabbing his belongings, another member of the government team entered the room. He was an Anglo male with a shaved head and tattoos that covered his arms. He was smoking from an e-cigarette, puffing his thick smoke in the air.

"How are you? I'm Brodi Sanders. Welcome to the team."

"Thanks, I'm Noah, RFP Writer."

"Cool, nice to meet you." He turned to address Robert Peterson, whom he'd missed so much, to update him on the team's progress. "Hey, Robert, I just connected with Richard Branson on CoWorker. I'm going to message him and ask if we can do a demo. Imagine if he decides to buy the company. We'd all be millionaires overnight."

"Richard Branson? The billionaire? Hey, it doesn't hurt to try," replied Robert, encouraging Brodi's ridiculous efforts.

What the fuck would he want to do with this place? Is this guy crazy? Pondered Noah.

"You're going after some massive fish," he said.

"Go hard or go home, buddy, hehe..." replied Brodi. Robert Peterson closed the office door as soon as Noah and Brodi left the room. He sat in his chair and fell asleep for the rest of the afternoon. His snoring could be heard by anyone who walked by the office. It wasn't the first or the last time that he slept at work. It was all he ever did. Albert's longtime buddy was an invested shareholder in the company. He didn't have to do anything except pretend like he was working.

Noah walked to the cubicle area in the back where the sales people were situated. He didn't make a fuss about the office he was promised but never received. Instead, he carried his belongings to an old, dusty cubicle that was located by the "back" doorways, although the entire floor was a round circle. The desk adjoined Mitch's cubicle without a central divider, making them workmates for the foreseeable future.

He found his new surroundings to be dreary and cold. There was no sun light because the panoramic windows ran along the Director's offices. The walls were painted yellow, and the cubicles were surrounded by old filing cabinets and furniture that Albert had hoarded. The area was also used to contain and isolate CannaTron's most volatile employee. She was the large, older woman with a short, boyish haircut who worked in sales. Her name was Helen Espinoza, and she was old-school tough. But more importantly, the woman was loud and unintelligent, and she cussed like a sailor.

It wasn't easy for Noah to introduce himself to Helen. Every time he walked passed her cubicle, she would slump over and stare at the computer screen. He knew she wasn't shy, so he concluded that she had already held something against him. Still, that didn't prevent Noah from getting to know her on a more personal level. He sat behind her and could hear everything that she said and did.

In the wait for the Washington RFP, Noah started a blog for the company and used his graduate school knowledge to focus on medical cannabis. It was a niche that he chose to help the company sound more credible and help generate traffic to the website. But other than that, he had plenty of time to observe Helen's tantrums.

"What the fuck is wrong with this thing? I swear, I'm gonna leave this place, and they'll be sorry. I'll have them begging me to come back!" She grumbled while angrily pounding on the keyboard.

"Hey, Aziz, are you in there!? I need a fucking computer that works, man!" said the deplorable woman. But Aziz was never in his office, causing her frustrations to grow.

The loud bursts of verbal excrement went on, day after day, without any repercussion. Jamie often got annoyed with Helen's challenged persona, especially with her inability to learn how to use a computer. But nobody detested Helen more than Mitch. He couldn't stand her and wished nothing more than for her to be fired.

Two weeks after Noah moved to the cubicle, Kenny arrived from a business trip in Oregon. He had hardly been there, in the office, since the day Noah arrived. Three days after arriving from Oregon, the Co-CEO finally decided to properly welcome Noah to the company. Helen, confused to hell with her computer, took advantage of his presence and quickly pulled Kenny to the side.

"Hey, Kenny! Do you think you can get me a computer? This shit's broken. I can't get into Sales Force with this cheap piece of crap," she said.

"Oh, I'm sorry to hear that, Helen. I thought we recently got you a new computer," said Kenny politely.

"For Christ's sake, Helen! How many times did I tell you this morning that Sales Force is down and it would be better to use your time making phone calls today!" said Jamie as she stormed from her desk to Helen's.

"I tried making phone calls today, but blondie keeps bitching at me because...," yelled Helen about Brittney.

"Shhh," said Jamie as she pointed to Noah.

"Oh, right, the new guy, sorry," whispered Helen. "But blondie keeps bitching at me to hand in last week's report, and I don't got nothing to show as long as Sales Force is down."

Noah was hysterical and could hardly contain his laughter. He was used to the antics and continued to write his blog article until Kenny finally arrived. "Hey, Noah, let's talk for a minute in my office."

Noah and Bryan Miller sat in Kenny's dimmed office while two massive golden retrievers rested behind his desk. The only light that entered the room was through a half-opened set of blinds. The Korcan/Amcrican, as always, lookcd cxhaustcd and disoriented. He kept the lights low to mask his poor appearance. But despite fatigue and a weak body frame, Kenny Cho stood tall and eloquent.

"Those are some nice dogs. Retrievers are very smart," said Noah.

"Yes, I know. They're my babies, Rocko and Bruce. The house is getting sprayed for bugs, so they'll be spending the day with me," said Kenny. Then he remembered something critical. He reached into a duffle bag to grab the dog's blanket and put it next to Rocko. "That's a good boy," he whispered while petting the dog on the head. Once that matter was addressed, he proceeded with the meeting. *What the fuck is wrong with this place?* thought Noah.

"Noah, Bryan, I'd like to start by apologizing for not being here this past month to properly introduce you to the company. I've been busy traveling. I'm busy now, and I'll be busy for the next month. But, I'd like to take some time to discuss our company vision, my vision," he said before pointing to a small map on the wall that looked like it was drawn by a kindergartener.

"This is the heat map. It's a little something I created to indicate the areas in the country where we want to set our focus. These states in orange are states where cannabis is legal. These states in blue are where we are currently present. And the yellow dots indicate states that will look to legalize in the next two years. As you can see, we have Oregon and New York state contracts. We're anticipating Washington and Nevada to release RFPs in the near future. Noah, that's why you are here. That's where you'll shine. We need you to manage the proposal, procure the data, and submit a thorough response. As our senior writer, we need you to make us look good," emphasized Kenny.

"Bryan, we're waiting for your Bar score. Until then, we feel that your experience in this industry will serve best on the government team. I was once a member of the government team. You'll work directly for our Director, Robert Peterson, alongside Brodi Sanders. Brodi has been with this company for three years on a part-time basis while managing Albert's medical clinics as well. How do you feel about this role?"

Before law school, Bryan Miller lived in California for four years, growing illegal pot in the mountains of Humboldt County. After the harvest season, he would ship the product back to Florida, where things were less progressive. To avoid leaving tracks, he would hire an illegal immigrant to mail a one-pound package without leaving a return address or sender name. The weed was compressed and tightly concealed in duct tape and plastic wrapping. The package was sent to one of multiple P.O. boxes that were set up by the receiver. It was a wild time for federal agents who were unable to control the massive amounts of deliveries being sent across the United States.

Bryan made a decent profit during that time, helping to flush the state with high-grade marijuana strains. He ultimately used the money to help pay for law school. With the knowledge that he gained and the connections he made in California, Bryan also started a small, non-profit website that brought awareness to the need for medical cannabis in Florida. Maybe he wasn't the best law student, but he was certainly a genius when it came to the fundamentals of the weed industry.

"Well, I know that Congressman Cleary has drafted a bill with other representative sponsors to add an excise tax on all cannabis sales in Washington. If this passes the committee, it could open the way for mandatory tracking," said Bryan.

"Exactly, it's like the wild west out there. My projection for the next five years is to obtain state contracts for California, Washington, Colorado, Texas, and Florida. If we can secure those states, then I feel that we can put ourselves in a strong position when legalization goes national," replied Kenny while pointing to the heat map.

Midway through the meeting, Ian and Brittney rudely gathered at Kenny's doorway. They stood smiling as Kenny spoke to Bryan and Noah, having little regard for the briefing. Noah thought it was unprofessional for them to intervene. He looked at Kenny to see how he would address the situation as CEO. But to his disappointment, it became apparent that Kenny and the two assistants were pals. He noticed the two standing at the door and remembered some old joke that they had shared. He smiled and asked, "What are you two doing?"

"Mr. Cho, I think you forgot about something that happened before you left," said Ian while swinging a little brown bag with two fingers. "Does a little wager ring a bell?"

"Ha! Ha! Ha! Oh no," replied Kenny. "What shirt did you pick out?"

"Ah, so you do remember," replied Brittney. "But don't worry, it's cute."

Ian handed Kenny the bag. In it was a pink t-shirt that read SAUCY across the chest. Kenny, all excited, put on the t-shirt over his dress shirt, basking in the humor of the inside joke. As far as the meeting was concerned, it was over.

"Look at you! It fits great," said Ian.

"I also got your suitcase over the weekend. Everything is ready for your flight tomorrow," said Brittney as she showed him the large suitcase.

"That's a nice one, spacious," said Kenny.

"Yeah, Kenny. I think it's big enough to fit you inside," said Ian.

"Do you think so?" asked Kenny, whose tone of voice changed from serious and professional to childish and giddy. "Well, let's see. I want to see."

Noah found the situation to be bizarre. In seven years of experience as a corporate writer, he'd never seen what was about to transpire, especially not from a CEO. It would be the moment when Noah lost total respect for the company.

Ian rested the suitcase on the floor and opened it. Kenny giggled like a little girl as he measured the sides with his hands like a true Asian prodigy.

"I think this is going to work," said Kenny.

He stepped into the suitcase and lay on his side in a fetal position. His tiny frame fit perfectly while Brittney and Ian encouraged him with their laughter. Noah was lost and confused and had no idea what was happening.

"What the fuck is this?" he gestured to Bryan Miller, who replied by shrugging his shoulders.

"Okay, now close it, close it," said Kenny.

Noah held down the suitcase as Ian and Bryan worked on the zippers. It closed without a problem.

"How does it feel?" asked Brittney.

"It's actually not that bad," echoed Kenny from inside the suitcase.

It was the only time that he would witness such behavior from Kenny. As a result, he concluded that his boss, who wore a wedding ring, was either a schizophrenic or a closet homosexual.

Later that day, Noah was at his cubicle writing a blog entry about the effects of medical marijuana on bone fracture healing. All the while, he tried to forget everything that'd happened in

Kenny's office. Thinking of that only made him feel miserable about where he worked. Just as he was finishing the blog, he suddenly found himself in the presence of Eugene Pierre, the company CTO. The large but delicate Haitian casually walked his way toward the back area and found himself alone with Noah.

"What's up, man?" asked Noah with a friendly undertone.

"Hey, I'm trying to find some honey. You got some?" said Eugene in a soft voice.

"Honey? No, sorry, I'm all out," replied Noah sarcastically.

"Really? That's not good," said a disappointed Eugene. He went as far as curling his lip and frowning.

"Um, I'll holla next time I got some," replied Noah to keep the humor light.

Eugene giggled and replied, "Hmm, you crazy, boy."

The CTO left the room to return to his office. At the same time, Noah heard a profound and unavoidable voice talking in the distance. He could hear a man joking, laughing, and getting reacquainted with some of the other employees. Noah sensed something unsettling about the man's laugh. It warned him of the nonsense that was to come.

Mark Smith flew in from Colorado that day to discuss business with Albert. The fifty-something-year-old walked into the office with a polo shirt and shorts, an exaggerated tan, and greasy, slicked hair. After greeting some of the support staff, he walked into Aziz's office to get reacquainted with his former co-worker.

"What's up, you Jihadi motherfucker? Thanks for bailing on me in Vegas," said Mark Smith with a Southern accent.

"You delinquents were about two seconds from getting arrested. That bouncer should have kicked your ass for sticking your finger in that stripper's ass," said Aziz.

"Well, hell, I paid her three hundred bucks! She was just uptight if you ask me," said Mark before smiling.

"I think you're right on that," said Aziz. "So, what's going on? How's the chamber going?"

"Well, you know, doing our best to influence the laws that are being written in Colorado. We're low on funding, so the guys got me back here to see if Albert wants to contribute," said Mark.

"Good fucking luck with that. The old man is at the end of his rope, and his patience is almost non-existent," replied Aziz. "I think he's in a meeting for the next hour, but I'm sure there's a place in the back where you can set up shop while you wait."

Mark Smith left Aziz's office and walked around the back area to look for a place to set up his laptop. He mumbled to himself in a low tone while searching for a power socket. After a senile moment, he noticed Noah sitting in his cubicle. He smiled with his bleached chompers and proceeded to introduce himself.

"Hello, I'm Mark Smith. Good to meet you," he said.

"Hi, I'm Noah, an RFP writer," replied Noah while shaking hands.

"Hey, you know if anyone's sitting here?" asked Mark while pointing to the lavish desk that rested against the back wall.

"I haven't seen anybody sit there in almost two months," replied Noah.

"Thanks," said Mark.

He pushed the desk off the wall and slid it forward to make room. After pulling up a chair, he rested his items on the desk and took a moment to catch his breath. It wasn't long before some of the other employees heard of his presence and went to see him. One by one, Jamie, Kristin, and Helen, some of the originals, arrived to greet their former co-worker.

"Hey, you dirty son of a bitch, haven't died from STDs yet!?" shouted Helen.

"No, I practice safe sex. I pull out each time!" replied the comical Mr. Smith. His laugh was just as loud as his personality.

"Hi, Mark. It's so good to see you. I miss you. This place isn't fun anymore," said Jamie.

"Aww, baby, I miss the fun we had too. But, wow, you're looking sexy. Wanna take a lunch break like we used to?" said Mark Smith as she pressed her tits against him with a strong hug.

"Nope, I don't fly that route anymore," said Jamie.

"Ah, so you're finally sticking to taco," responded Mark before laughing.

"Yep, less stress, softer touch," said Jamie.

Mark Smith was a middle-aged, sexually defiant cocaine addict. He left his sales position at CannaTron to help form the National Marijuana Chamber of Commerce in Colorado. They were a group comprised of old stoners and dirty business professionals who thought they could influence legislation in Colorado, hoping to eventually control the direction of the industry. They attempted to draft bills and influence politicians, but the committee was a joke. It was full of pretentious miscreants who hardly worked and didn't know shit about the compliance laws. Nobody who mattered in the industry took them seriously.

"Hi, Mark," said Ian in his gayest voice.

"What's up, baby? You're looking sexy," replied Mark.

What the fuck? Did he really just say that? thought Noah as he worked quietly, though eavesdropping.

"I'm still mad at you for eating my cake without my permission," said Ian with a ratchet expression on his face.

"It was a fun night. There was cake everywhere, baby," replied Mark without any concern about who was listening.

"Yes, but you promised that you would behave. I woke up and just saw your face there, eating away," replied Ian with a deep yet devilish laugh.

I know these motherfuckers aren't talking about food, thought Noah, who pretended like he wasn't listening.

"So, am I going to see you tonight? I fly back to Colorado early in the morning," said Mark.

"Who are you going to be with?" asked Ian.

"Probably just Albert, Delfino, and Lee," replied Mark.

"Oh, God, no; please, not Lee, that guy has issues," said Ian.

"Lee is a fun guy. Just come out to dinner, and we'll all head back to Albert's place," said Mark.

"I don't know. Lee can get kinda nuts," replied Ian.

"C'mon, we'll all take turns passing you around like the good old days," said Mark with a devilish smile.

Noah wasn't surprised by what he heard, just further disappointed about his workplace. He didn't agree with the content of the conversation, not in a place where anyone could hear. He endured it for as long as he could before quietly leaving through the back doors.

Noah arrived downstairs and walked outside through the building doors. He was surprised to find Albert moping next to two supercharged Jaguar XJs that were parked at the building entrance. One was black, and the other was red. He purposefully displayed both cars at the entrance for everyone to notice his riches.

"Wow, those are some beautiful machines," said Noah, who felt inclined to say something to his boss.

"Thank you, Noah. Are you a car enthusiast?" said Albert as the Florida sun beamed onto his face.

"I used to be. But I never owned anything like those," said Noah. Albert looked deeply at both cars before replying, "I used to have seven of them. These are the only two left."

"I'm sorry to hear that. What happened?" asked Noah.

Albert looked to the pavement, then to the car, and said, "I got divorced. Don't ever get married." He burst out laughing and officially made the moment awkward.

"Sounds like good advice. I'll see you later, Albert," said Noah before walking to his car.

After an extended lunch, he returned to work and was relieved to see that Mark was gone. There was a hostile commotion coming out of Aziz's office. He could hear a shouting match between Aziz and Helen. She was being reprimanded because a customer complained about her use of foul language.

"Helen, at no point are you supposed to say the words "Fuck off" to any of our customers! When will you get it through your fucking head that you can't mouth off every time you feel like it!?" yelled Aziz.

"You know what? I don't even know why I'm fucking listening to you! You're not my boss. Albert is!" said the always defiant Helen.

"I'm your boss! I'm Chief Operating Officer, and I run the department! If I feel you need to go, you're out!"

"Well, fine, whatever, but Albert's not going to get rid of me. I was here before everyone. When other assholes were complaining to him, oh, I hate my job, oh, you don't pay enough, I kept my mouth shut. And he appreciated that. He told me once. But if you're gonna threaten me, then I'll just take it up with him."

"You're walking on a thin, fucking line. Do it again, and you're fired!" shouted Aziz.

Helen stormed out the door and straight to her cubicle to grab a cigarette. The other sales girls, Jamie and Kristin, abandoned their posts to smoke with her and make sure she was okay. A minute later, Aziz came out of his office with an intense look on his face.

"Did Helen go outside?" he asked Noah.

"Uh, I think so. I think they all went to have a cigarette," replied Noah.

Aziz left the office through the back doors with his pack of Marlboros. Seconds later, Brittney walked to the back- area and saw that Aziz's door was closed. She turned to Noah and said, "What happened? Is everything okay?"

"Aziz and Helen got in a fight. Then they both went outside to smoke cigarettes," replied Noah.

"God, I'm sorry you had to see that. I'm sorry I didn't warn you about Helen, but she's kinda loud. That's why we had you sitting on the other side near me. We even told her to watch her language when you came, and like, stay away from you. But don't worry. We're figuring out this whole office situation. I really appreciate that you're cool with this. It's only temporary," said Brittney.

"That's funny. But don't worry about me. I'm fine right here for now," said Noah.

"Okay, I'm going downstairs to see if everything is alright. Do you smoke?"

"Only when I'm drunk. But no, not normally," replied Noah.

"My ex-husband was like that. I think I only saw him smoke a few times," said Brittney while chewing gum, twirling her hair, and staring at Noah like a piece of meat.

"What happened?" asked Noah. "You said was."

"He died two years ago in a car accident. It's just our son and me now," she replied.

"I'm sorry for your loss, Brittney."

"It's fine. I mean, I feel sorry for my son, who will never know his real dad. As far as the relationship, it was never good. And after

Alex died, things got nasty with his parents. They were all focused on his money and his trust fund, and his assets. They took me to court, but I eventually told them to take everything. I couldn't afford all those court fees. They even wanted my son, claiming that I was an unfit mother. In the end, it's just me with a kid. But at least I don't have to worry about those people."

"Good for you," replied Noah, who got an insight into her dark soul.

"Yeah, right?" she said before a brief pause. "Sorry, I didn't mean to bombard you with all of this."

"No, worries, I'm glad to see you're doing well," said Noah.

"So, I was wondering, do you know anything about speakers? I just had two speakers and a subwoofer installed in my new CRV, and I need someone to check if it sounds good. You want to help me out?" asked Brittney.

This chick totally wants to fuck in her car, thought Noah. It was all that his male mind allowed him to think.

"It sounds like fun, but I don't think my fiancé would appreciate that," he said despite being flattered by her advances.

"Whoa, take it easy, Romeo. I was just asking you about my speakers. I didn't say anything about sex," replied Brittney while smiling.

"Who said anything about sex? Where's your mind at, Ms. Brittney?" said Noah in a playful manner.

By the end of the day, the wackiness had dissipated. Helen was an emotional wreck, and Brittney convinced her to go home for the day to help ease the overall tension at work. Aziz, worried about maintaining low employee turnover, called Noah into his office to make sure he wasn't bothered. He didn't want to lose his copywriter after only a couple of months.

"What's up, boss?" said Noah.

"Take a seat, man," said Aziz with his hands folded on the desk. "I'm sorry you had to see all that. As you can see, Helen is a special case. She's good at pulling in sales, but she has no concept of courtesy or respect. Are you okay?"

"I'm fine. Don't worry about me. I'm good. I really enjoy learning all this stuff about pot and the industry. I can tell you got your hands full. But I was wondering, how did you get into all of this?" asked Noah.

"I'm actually a licensed pharmacist. I ran my own pharmacy in Miami for ten years, and Albert used to run a wellness clinic here in Fort Lauderdale. So, this isn't our first venture together. One day he brought the CannaTron idea to me, asking me for help, and I liked his offer. So, I sold my pharmacy to some Cubans and jumped on the pot train."

"I'm sure, as a pharmacist, you're a real asset to Albert," said Noah.

"Yeah, it's a credible title whenever we talk to growers or doctors. I also spent a lot of time in Colorado over the years. I got really familiar with the industry and made a lot of good connections while I was there," said Aziz.

"I can't even begin to imagine what it's like over there," said Noah.

"It's pretty amazing. This one time, I went to a storage

warehouse to meet this guy who supposedly had a new hybrid strain to sell. Well, I arrived at the place, and there were people who had set up shop and were selling pots from their storage units. And let me tell you. They were here pulling in thousands of dollars a day. I mean, with recreational pots becoming legal, a lot of people got rich. And once all that shit is tracked and accounted for, the state will report billions of dollars in tax revenue. It's really interesting to see how things have progressed over the years."

"Ha, wow, I learn something new every day in this place," said Noah.

"Well, look, I just wanted to make sure that you were alright. I don't want Helen scaring you away before the Washington RFP even comes. So, if you'll excuse me, I need to discuss a pending lawsuit with E-Greens."

"Who's E-Greens?" asked Noah. "I've heard that name around the office a few times."

"They're the competition. Right now, they're just mad 'cause we're two-for-two on state contracts. They're suing us for false advertisement, but it's just sour apples," said Aziz.

"What's the difference between our product and E- Greens?" asked Noah.

"Um, well, for one thing, our system uses an RFID scanner to track the plants. Their product uses a barcode scanner which isn't as reliable. Our system also provides a transportation manifest for all shipments. And we also have a patented A.P.I. that syncs directly to the government monitoring system. Nobody else has that. Technically, E-Greens was the first company to offer cannabis tracking, but we were the first to create and patent the

A.P.I."

Noah left work after his meeting with Aziz. He was slowly getting fed up with CannaTron's antics and knew that he had to locate a new job. It became his intention to achieve that or leave within the month. Just before he got into his car, his phone rang.

"Hello?" said Noah.

"Hello, Noah. How are you? This is Dr. Patel from the university."

"Dr. Patel! Good to hear from you. How can I help you?" asked Noah.

"Noah, there's no good way to say this, but you fell short of the minimal graduation GPA by .025 points. Your final GPA as of now is 3.175. As you know, the minimal GPA to graduate is 3.2," revealed Dr. Patel.

"So, I got an A on my final, but it still wasn't enough?" replied Noah.

"Correct, Noah, I'm sorry. And I'm sorry about the delay with the grades. Two of our professors left unexpectedly after finals last semester, and we've been trying to catch up." The news meant that Noah was ineligible to apply to medical school for the upcoming term. He would have to wait another year before he could submit his applications.

"So, what's my next step?" asked Noah, who took a deep breath to absorb the unfortunate news.

"Well, there is a solution. Next semester you can take a course that's worth one credit. You don't have to show up for class or anything. But you will be required to write a research paper that will be published in a medical journal. How does that sound to you?"

"It's better than nothing. But I'm not sure what to write," replied Noah.

"Come into my office next week, and we will discuss some topics. Does that sound okay?" said Dr. Patel.

"Yes, Doctor, thanks again," said Noah.

Noah sat in his cubicle for the next couple of days with little motivation to do anything. He'd fallen into a light state of depression after finding out that he wouldn't graduate that semester. To make things worse, Mitch returned to the office after attending a Cannabis event in Oregon. Outside of those trade shows, he virtually became useless to the company. He spent his time creating branding tasks for himself with no marketing budget and no creativity. He also made sales calls because his replacement had yet to be hired. Kristin, the hippie sales girl, heard of Mitch's arrival and walked from her area to greet him.

"Hi, guys; Hi, Mitch," said Kristen.

"Hey," said Mitch with a disinterested tone.

It was common knowledge at work that she had a crush on him. Despite her attractiveness, Mitch had no interest in her advances. No matter how many times she walked across his desk without a bra, exposing her skinny-girl breasts through a tight shirt, Mitch completely ignored her.

"Hi, Kristen. You look nice today," said Noah.

"Thanks, Noah. You're not too shabby yourself," she replied. "Hey, Mitch, are you going bowling with us after work?" she asked.

"Uh, no, I can't," replied Mitch, who refused to make eye contact with Kristin. As usual, he rudely continued to stare at the computer as she spoke.

"You can't, or you won't?" replied Kristen.

"Uh, more like I don't want to," said Mitch.

"Why not? I'll be there. Don't you want to hang?" asked Kristen.

"Haven't I told you that I have a girlfriend?"

"Uh, Mitch, you're no fun," said Kristen in a disappointed tone. "Noah, come by if you want. It'll be fun," said Kristen before leaving the office to have a cigarette.

While sitting at his desk, biting his nails, and figuring out how to write, as well as Noah, Mitch decided to go on a rant.

"Oh, fuck," he said to himself, hoping that Noah heard.

"What's wrong?" asked Noah, who hadn't forgotten about the way Mitch tried to sabotage his work.

"I just got an email from Debbie. She forgot to file my expenses for this upcoming paycheck. I sent her the invoice two nights ago, and she said she had forgotten. That fucking bitch! I can't take this anymore. We can't keep functioning like this. Kenny needs to get his ass here from wherever he's at and clean house, starting with fucking Brittney and working his way down. We got stock coming our way, fucking up at work fucks with my money. And nobody's going to fuck with my money," said Mitch.

"Take it easy, Walsh," replied Noah.

"No, I'm sorry, I can't. Every day, it's something new with these people. But once Kenny takes full control, he'll get rid of these monkeys. I mean, have you realized how much of a fucking bitch Brittney is? Like, have you seen the way she treats people? I swear, Elaine can sue her for emotional abuse if she really wants to. She walks around like she is all high and mighty, but she doesn't do anything. She always complains about all the work she has. Since when is it hard to book airplane flights on the internet?" vented Mitch.

"I didn't tell you. I had the pleasure of meeting Mark Smith while you were away," said Noah.

"Oh, no. I can't stand that fucking guy."

"I thought he was somebody important. At least, that's how he projects himself," said Noah.

"Fuck that guy. He's nobody. He used to work in sales when I got here. One day, I was complaining about how we weren't documenting any of these sales, and he told me to stop acting like a fucking baby. I almost quit that day."

"So, what does he do now?" asked Noah.

"He's a member of that National Marijuana Chamber of Commerce, which is total bullshit. Nobody gives a fuck about that organization. I'm telling you, once these jokers are gone, we can finally start getting to work at this place. We won't have to deal with the abuse, with the cigarette breaks, with the inconsistencies. And we won't have to deal with this buddy system they think they have with Kenny."

"What buddy system?" asked Noah.

"Haven't you noticed? They call themselves the ratchet crew; Kenny, Brittney, Ian, Debbie, Jamie, Brodi, and Kristin. They think because they're friends with Kenny that they have some type of seniority in this place."

"I thought seniority was based on experience, education, and position," said Noah.

"Pffft, education? Other than Zack, Bryan, and myself, none of the assholes you see in the office have a college degree."

Standing at the doorway of his office, Zack Stansbury intervened. He didn't disagree with what he was hearing. But everybody in the office knew that Mitch was a whiner, a complainer.

"Mitch Walsh, what the hell are you talking about this time?"

"I'm talking about how fucked up it is the way some people get away with murder at this place."

"Awe, what's the matter, baby? Big, bad, Brittney got you down?" jokingly mocked Zack.

"We gotta take this industry by the balls, and as long as we have people like that here, it won't happen. Hell, you want your stock money, right, Zack?"

"Of course, I want my money. But I tell you what you really need to be worried about...," said Zack before farting while smiling and staring Noah in the eyes.

Just as the stench traveled through the air, Bryan Miller walked out of his office while holding one of his mother's gourmet sandwiches.

"Zack, did you rip ass?" he asked.

"Indeed, my challenged friend. Get used to it 'cause I'm going to be farting up a storm at the racquetball court. See you at six at the gym," said Zack before leaving for the restroom.

"Hey, homie," said Bryan to Noah. "Try these out. I got them in Colorado over the weekend. It's pot taffy, an edible. I took two at my friends' wedding, and I was just gone for the rest of the night. This wedding had a dab bar for the guests, but I was so high off the edible that I couldn't smoke anymore. I suggest you take it in moderation. Have a piece every fifteen minutes. That way, you'll get a nice, chill high."

After that bizarre week, Noah could use a strong high. He felt like he'd won a small lottery and couldn't wait to take the candy in the comfort of his own home. Although the drugs were appreciated, he never imagined that a co-worker would give him drugs on work premises. But that was simply the reality of his life. There was no place for decency at CannaTron.

Chapter 5
The Real History of Albert Abraham and CannaTron

2006 - Fort Lauderdale, Florida

The Sun Valley Center for Pain Management was a *Center of Excellence and Compassion for the Fort Lauderdale Community.* At least, that's what the sign on the front door read. It was situated quaintly in a Publix shopping center not too far from the beach. The clinic promised medical care and adequate treatment to addicts who'd entered a drug-recovery program. But in the early and mid-2000s, places like that were all just a cover-up.

The establishment was funded and managed by Dr. Albert Abraham, Ph.D. He partnered with a licensed physician who ran the clinic during Florida's infamous pill-mill era. Along with workers like Brodi Sanders and other questionable characters, Abraham's team distributed painkillers to addicts without strict regulations or government oversight because they didn't exist at the time.

The state of Florida didn't have a statewide prescription-drug monitoring program. People like Abraham and his cronies pushed drugs like Oxycontin, Methadone, Xanax, and Valium into the streets and made a fortune. With guys like Aziz Bashir on his payroll, Albert made millions, charging patients $250 dollars, cash, per visit, without the need for insurance. Apart from that, the low-lives that he hired to run the front desk took their share by selling prescription pads and other services under the table without Albert knowing.

Patients fed their addictions until they died, and nobody cared. When a death occurred, the coroner's office would find the pill bottle with the patient's name and clinic information and call the front desk to verify the body. The death count in Florida grew to an epidemic level because of people like Albert, who got rich off the weak and ill.

The clinic ran at high capacity, full of addicts jonesing for their pills. They became the living dead, possessed beings who'd lost all sense of decency. They would get into fights in the waiting room, snort pills in the bathroom, and perform sexual favors for drugs. There was never a physical examination, urine examination, or any type of care package offered to the patients. The addicts would simply pay their fees and walk away with their prescriptions.

Eventually, the Florida Department of Health and the DEA caught on to the scandal and raided the clinic. They raided clinics all over the state in a massive operation, taking files, computers, and other items considered to be evidence. Although raids were being conducted all over the country, Florida was considered ground zero by Federal agents.

Albert's staff physician was arrested, and the Florida Board of Medicine found him guilty of excessively prescribing pain medications. Albert was also detained by officials, but he easily set bail and was released within a few hours. There was a mountain of evidence against both conspirators, enough to put them away for a long time. That's why it was a mystery to many that neither was criminally charged.

Albert paid their way to freedom. He was a business associate with members of the Florida Bar Commission and once sat on the board of Bethesda Hospital in Broward County. He was filthy rich, highly connected, and used those connections to get away with murder. After the ordeal, he took what was left of his millions and walked away from the illegal pharmaceutical industry.

But Albert wasn't finished. He was a serial entrepreneur. In the wake of the pill-mill scandal, he saw an opportunity to capitalize on his experiences. He patented technologies that tracked prescription painkillers and helped place a regulatory system in the state. He started to track the same pills that he used to sell illegally. Of course, he didn't manufacture the technology. He only paid somebody to do it.

AJ Lauria was the true genius behind Albert's success in the software industry. He was a skinny, anti-social college dropout who was unemployed and almost completely bald before the age of thirty. He spent all his time in front of his computer, hidden in his room, in his mother's apartment. The day that he met Albert was the day that his life would change forever.

AJ and Albert lived on opposite sides of the country when they first met, Albert in Florida and AJ in California. At the time, Albert was selling auto-dialers online and committing credit card fraud with the personal information he obtained from customers.

AJ was in line to be Albert's next victim when he called to purchase one of the auto-dialers. He ran into an ad that Albert posted online and called the number that was provided. They ended up talking about software programming and how AJ once had a job as a coder in Silicon Valley. The very next day, Albert flew AJ to Florida and pitched his idea to create the painkiller tracking software that was eventually named SequenceRX. AJ returned to California and wrote the code within three months. Albert patented the final product and had it audited by an independent firm before presenting it to government officials.

Albert was later proclaimed a hero in the war on drugs. He was invited to the governor's mansion and honored by Governor Jeb Bush and President George Bush Jr. He was accredited for being a key player in the reformation of laws pertaining to opiate regulation. Not long after that, the idea came to him to apply the same technology to legal marijuana.

While visiting a cannabis trade show in Colorado, he noticed that there were businesses trying to convince the government of their legitimacy but had no way to demonstrate compliance. Ultimately, he learned that the industry suffered from two fundamental problems. The first was the absence of banking options. No bank in the country was willing to provide loans to purchase and grow a federally illegal drug. The second was the absence of tracking technology that created auditing reports. That set the plan in motion, and he attended Oaksterdam University in California to study the cannabis plant while AJ wrote the code for the new system.

But Albert didn't have enough capital to start the new operation. At least, that's what he claimed. So, he partnered with investor and lover Frank Delfino and high school friend Robert Peterson. They formed a board and hired a handful of cheap minions to initiate their daily business operations. That marked the official birth of CannaTron.

Noah's instincts were right from the moment he entered the doors of the company. Without knowing anything about Albert's past, he sensed that it was riddled with scandal and indecency. He wasn't a CannaTron soldier like the other employees, like Mitch, Brittney, or Kenny. He didn't accept the policy that there were no vacation days or sick days, no insurance offerings, or no opportunities for professional advancement. But he wasn't a sucker and wouldn't let his time there go in vain. Without ever being planned, CannaTron presented him with the solution that he needed to finish graduate school.

Noah drove to the University campus to talk to Dr. Patel about the extra course he needed to graduate. After having researched and written multiple blogs about medicinal cannabis at CannaTron, it was easy for him to pick a topic. He wasn't sure if the University would approve his idea, but he was going to take an honest approach.

He found Dr. Patel having a conversation on the phone. The Dean waived his former student to enter and sit in a chair.

"Alright, okay, I'll make sure to have those to you by the end of the day. Thank you, goodbye," said Dr. Patel before hanging up the phone.

"Hello, Noah. Thank you for coming. I would like to discuss the research paper. As I said, it's a one-credit course, but if you complete the task, you will get an A and achieve the overall minimal GPA. Your paper will also be published in a medical journal which improves your chances of getting accepted to a medical program. Are there any particular areas that interest you?" asked Dr. Patel.

"Actually, there is; I'd like to write about medical marijuana. I currently work at a software company in the marijuana industry as a proposal writer, and I've had a lot of exposure to articles that discuss the current research and challenges that the industry faces," said Noah.

"I think that is an excellent topic. If you can gather enough information and provide an overall review of the current state of the industry, I think that'll be excellent. After that, I will work to publish the article in a medical journal. As I said, this is something that will greatly boost your chances of getting into a medical program."

The Dean's approval gave Noah a much-needed boost of confidence. He no longer saw his shortcomings as a barrier to success. Instead, he saw everything as an opportunity. It was an opportunity to stand out from other applicants by doing what he did best, write. He drove back to work with a renewed sense of energy, ready to conquer the task. His plans for leaving the company would have to be delayed. He would have to endure the daily circus that was CannaTron until the paper was finished.

Back at the office, Zack and Bryan had been building a friendship based on friendly competition. It started out with sports like racquetball, basketball, and even weightlifting. They would play one-on-one games or see who could lift the most reps at a nearby gym during their lunch break. The winner would always flaunt victory, and the loser would always be sour and have an excuse. Eventually, Zack injured his ankle in a parking lot race, and Bryan accused him of being a habitual cheater.

Once the early-thirty-somethings were done reliving their high school days, the sports competition evolved with bad intentions. It all started one day when Zack felt another putrid fart building up in his gut after a heavy lunch of eggplant parmesan and gnocchi.

He conjured a belligerent idea after another long night of drinking at Tootsie's.

Zack wanted to share the fart with someone special who could appreciate the effort, or so he thought. Noah watched him stumble out of his office, face flushed as usual, and straight into Bryan's office. He stood in front of Bryan's desk and just stared at him with an emotionless expression. Without saying a word, Zack unleashed an extended fart. Then he turned around, wafted in the air, and left the room. It took a few seconds for Bryan to process what had happened.

"Gross! Did you just shit yourself?" asked Bryan. A few seconds later, the smell reached his vicinity. "Aw, God, it stinks!"

Bryan covered his nose to avoid the smell. He stood up from his desk and ran to the closed door, which Zack had locked on his way out. Bryan struggled to turn the handle. When he finally did, he ran to Zack's office and found him sunk in his chair, laughing hysterically.

"Very funny, Stansbury. It'll be my pleasure to get you back, homie."

"Aww, poor baby Miller. Did I hurt the baby's feelings?" mocked Zack in typical fashion.

Bryan left the office with a determined grin and said while walking away, "You'll be sorry." He then turned to Noah, who found everything hilarious and said, "You're a witness. He started it."

A war had commenced, one that neither participant expected to lose. With no legitimate authority on site, they were free to battle without fear of repercussion. Albert and Kenny were rarely seen.

AJ Lauria worked from home. And Robert Peterson was asleep most of the time. Technically, Aziz was in charge, but he was spending too much time dealing with daily operations.

Later that afternoon, Zack stepped out of the office for a second lunch break. Bryan found it to be a perfect moment to retaliate for the putrid fart. He watched Zack from his office window as he got into his BMW. As soon as he drove off the parking lot, Bryan walked to Zack's office and started meddling with Zack's desk chair.

"What the fuck are you doing?" asked Noah while standing at the doorway of Zack's office.

"Payback. I hope he busts his ass when he takes a seat," said Bryan as he unfastened the final screw. He continued to place the chair at an angle where it would hold until the moment Zack sat on it. "There, that should do it. He ruined my lunch, and now I'll ruin his."

Zack returned to the office, anxious to eat his delicious Publix sub, having forgotten about the target on his back. Noah and Bryan waited quietly at their desks, listening for the moment when the chair broke. Zack was completely clueless as he put his sandwich on the desk and stretched his arms. Without thinking of any consequence, he sat down. The chair broke apart immediately, and Zack fell backward, breaking a hole through the drywall.

Zack immediately knew who was at fault, and he yelled out, "Bryan! What the hell is wrong with you? I could have broken my back!"

Bryan didn't deny that he was responsible. As soon as he heard Zack yell, he walked to the office and gave his trademark laugh.

"Bffffffft..."

"You're so dead, dude. You have no idea what's waiting for you. Be ready at all times, 'cause shit's about to go down," said Zack, who was checking the back of his head for blood.

"Aww, poor baby Zacky not happy? Pffft, fuck you," said Bryan while flipping the bird. "Bring it on, bitch."

Zack didn't waste any time executing his revenge. The next day, he got to work an hour early to monitor Bryan's arrival. As soon as Bryan entered the parking lot, he ran to the lawyer's office and put clear glue on all the office supplies, the chair, the phone, the mouse, and even his pens. When Zack was done, he walked out of Bryan's office with a big smile on his face, turned to Noah, and said, "You don't say shit."

"Hey, I'm just a quiet observer," replied Noah, who was setting up his computer for the morning. But by opening his mouth, he automatically became an active participant.

A minute later, the key-card reader chimed, and Bryan entered the office like it was any other day. He whistled a tune while wearing shades that he'd gotten at an EDM festival.

"Good morning, sir," he said to Noah.

"Sup, man," replied Noah.

"Captain Dipshit here?" asked Bryan about Zack.

Noah just pointed at Zack's door, which was open. Bryan took notice and continued straight to his office. He knew that retaliation from Zack was imminent, but he didn't expect it so soon. Bryan thought that Zack would be more cerebral about the matter.

He walked into his office and didn't notice anything unusual. He put down his bag and saw a drafted bill from some Boston Democrat on his desk. Attached to it was a note from Robert Peterson, which read: *Look this over. What are the licensee regs?*

As he read the details, Bryan sat down without noticing the glue on the chair. It didn't take long for him to realize that he'd been pranked.

"What the fuck?" he said quietly before reaching to feel what was on the chair. He observed the residue on his fingers and instantly knew what it was.

"Is this glue?" he asked himself.

Noah was at his desk when he heard Bryan say out loud, "Ha, Ha, nice one, Zack. Putting glue on my chair, real fucking mature."

Zack strutted out of his office with a huge smile on his face and looked at Noah, laughing. Bryan attempted to wipe his backside but concluded that it was a useless effort. He heard Zack laughing and proceeded to confront him.

"Uh, I think we're even for almost crippling me," said Zack. "Don't you think?"

Bryan came out of his office while wiping his hands and said, "Shit just got real."

Zack laughed hysterically and sarcastically at Bryan's threats.

"Dude, I'm the king of pranks. You're going to regret starting with me," said Zack.

"Starting with you? You came into my office and ripped ass. No, this is war, Zack. This is war," replied Bryan.

The office door opened, and Mitch Walsh entered the room wearing his aviators, a coat, and a tie. He looked dapper for a guy who only got paid a salary of forty thousand a year. He'd just arrived from another cannabis show in Boston and wasn't in the mood to witness the silliness. He stared at the mess of papers and other crap that he'd left on his desk and then noticed Zack and Bryan's quarrel.

"What's going on with them?" he asked Noah.

"They've been pulling pranks on each other this week."

Mitch rolled his eyes. He couldn't help it. He was a dedicated employee, uptight, somewhat cynical, but definitely an asshole. Nobody liked him, but he couldn't care less. Mitch was only determined to push his agenda and vision on Aziz, which included firing a lot of people and attaining an actual marketing budget. He felt the non-stop shenanigans only hindered the company's success and the potential to make millions. In essence, Mitch was living in a fantasy world because he truly loved the cannabis industry and thought that Albert would make him a millionaire.

"When will this bullshit end?" said Mitch.

"Good morning to you, too," said Noah.

"Sorry, man, but I hate walking into this place and seeing people joke around and NOT DO WORK! There are seven people downstairs smoking cigarettes who should be here doing sales and other shit."

"Who was down there?" asked Noah.

"Who do you think? The whole fucking ratchet crew," answered Mitch.

"Yeah, I notice that they take as many cigarette breaks as they want. But Aziz is an executive, how come he doesn't stop it?" asked Noah.

"Because Aziz doesn't know what the fuck he's doing. He has no control over the sales team, no strategy, and he's usually out there too. I mean, seriously, what the fuck is a COO anyway?" said Mitch.

At that point, Albert's council, Jerry Levine, arrived at his office. He was as unorthodox of a Jew as one could find. He was a hippie and a white-lion Rastafarian. True to his persona, his hair was long, his beard was thick, and he couldn't give two shits about the clothes he wore. As he unlocked the door to his office, Mitch said, "Isn't that true, Jerry?"

"I don't know what you're talking about, but if it's what I think you're talking about, yes, this whole place is fucked," said Jerry in an ascertained tone before opening the door. "Have a wonderful day, gentlemen," he said before walking into his office.

"I didn't realize you felt that way about Aziz. It always seems like you two work well together," said Noah.

"Well, he's my boss, and I have to try and do a good job no matter what. But this place never really invested in quality people like you. And up until now, these assholes have really slowed our progress. He spends too much time babysitting them. Nobody knows what the fuck they're doing," ranted Mitch.

Mitch's best friend at the company, Charlie Zimmerman, stepped into the conversation. He was an implementation specialist for the company and one of CannaTron's original employees.

"What are you talking about, Aziz?"

"Yes," replied Mitch.

"You should have seen the mess we were in yesterday. We got slammed with tickets around 1 pm because the servers went down in Oregon again. And instead of following the recovery plan that we implemented, Aziz had the new hires in tech support help the level 3 customers. They had no idea what they were doing, and neither did Aziz. Everything was fucked. I've been stuck doing damage control all morning."

"You see what I'm talking about, Noah. A successful business shouldn't function this way," said Mitch.

Suddenly, Eugene appeared and awkwardly intervened in the conversation. And once again, the company CTO had a lost and confused look on his face when he said, "Hey, Noah, did you ever get some of that honey?"

"No, sorry, Eugene. I didn't stock up," replied Noah sarcastically without being rude. "I'll make sure to email you once my supply comes in."

Eugene smiled and laughed, almost in a flirtatious kind of way.

"You're cute, but I need some for my tea. I always forget it at home."

Noah didn't feel threatened. Like Ian, Eugene was obviously gay by the will of God. There was no denying it.

"Sorry, man. But I seriously don't have any," said Noah. Eugene gave a pouty face and walked away.

Charlie looked at Noah and said, "What the hell was that?"

"I have no idea. He's always coming around here asking me for honey," replied Noah while shrugging his shoulder. "So, anyway, who hired these people that you hate so much?"

At that moment, Charlie looked at Mitch, laughed, and said, "You want to tell him about Tommy?"

Mitch looked at Noah and said, "There used to be a guy who worked here. His name was Tom Parsons, Tommy. He was the VP of Sales. The guy was a fucking whack job and a meth addict. His dealers even came here one day looking for him, threatening to kill us if they didn't get their money."

"What the fuck?" replied Noah.

"Wait, it gets better," replied Charlie. "I walked into his office once, and he was snorting pills off his desk. He tried to brush it off and act casual, but his nose was covered in powder. There was no way that he could hide it. He started to talk to me about some sales reports with amphetamines all over his face. It was the funniest fucking thing that I'd ever seen. After a couple of minutes, I had to stop him, and I told him to go to the bathroom to clean his face."

"Forget that," said Mitch. "This asshole disappeared from work one day and went on a drug binge for a month. Just like that, he left. At some point, he even tried to break into the office to rob the place. He broke the handle on the side door but still couldn't get in. We saw everything on the cameras. A few weeks after that, he just returned to work as if nothing happened," said Mitch.

"And nobody said anything?" asked Noah.

Mitch and Charlie only looked at him and shrugged their shoulders.

"Who the fucked hired this guy?" continued Noah.

"Yeah, so Albert hired Tom, who hired Ian, Brittney, Helen, Jamie, Kristin, and Debbie. They all used to throw full-blown parties in the conference room with shots and all kinds of drugs," said Charlie to Noah. "Remember Kenny's party when Kristin told us she was a stripper?" said Charlie to Mitch.

"What happened at Kenny's party?" asked Noah, who was becoming overwhelmed with the revelations about the company.

"Oh yea. This guy, Tom, decided to order a stripper for Kenny's birthday. So, we all sat in the conference room while this stripper was dry-humping Kenny on the table, and David turned to me and said something like, *This stripper is useless. She doesn't even take off her clothes.* Mind you, David's gay," whispered Mitch.

"Kristin heard that, and she flipped out. She yelled at him, saying that strippers were people like everyone else and he had no right to judge her," further explained Mitch.

"So, it really hit home. But did she actually say she was a stripper?" asked Noah, who was humored and wanted to hear more details.

"Yeah, she started crying, and I asked her what was wrong. She told me that David's comments offended her because she was a stripper for two years and understood the shit they go through," said Charlie.

"Helen is the worst of all. She's everything that's wrong with this place all rolled into one person. I worked sales with her for six months, and her mouth should have gotten her fired a long time ago. Have you heard some of the shit she says? She's like almost sixty and still acts like a fucking child," said Mitch.

At that moment, the doors opened, and the sales girls, Brittney and Aziz, marched into the office with a renewed sense of energy. They brought a thick stench of tobacco into the room.

"C'mon, everybody, let's do some work," said Aziz. At that moment, Mitch went into kiss-ass mode with Aziz after talking bad about him, exposing his two-sided nature.

"Aziz, I think I know how we can fuck over E-Greens' marketing strategy in Washington. But I need your approval on this."

"What's up, man? What-choo-got?" replied Aziz, who always appreciated dirty play.

"So, Charlie noticed that these fuckers created a customized website for the Washington customers. I guess they're trying to personalize themselves in the market," said Mitch as he scrolled through the page.

"Oh, shit, they're copying our strategy," replied Aziz.

"I mean, the page sucks, but they at least have compliance laws as we do," said Mitch.

"Right, right, we need to find a way to revert this information," said Aziz.

"Exactly! I love the way you think. That's what I wanted to show you," said Mitch. "The domain name is egreenswa.com. But the domain name egreenwa.com is still available. They never bought it. I did. Now I want to revert that domain to our Washington web page. Every time someone spells it wrong, we'll get that traffic. What do you think?" said Mitch.

"Damn, Walsh, keeping it gangster," said Charlie.

"Na, fuck that, I love it," said Aziz. "Link your domain to our Washington page. That's how we roll at CannaTron, with some gangster-ass shit."

Everyone went back to their own tasks. Noah turned to his computer, opened his inbox, and saw an e-mail from Kenny. It was sent to the proposal team and the executive employees. The subject line read [Washington State RFP]. The proposal from the Washington State Liquor and Cannabis Board had arrived. Kenny attached it and sent links to a project management application that he wanted to use for the proposal development process. He gave Noah instructions to review the entire package and create a response matrix.

Kenny finished the email explaining that he would be in Oregon testifying for CannaTron in the E-Greens lawsuit and wasn't sure when he would return. Noah was concerned that he was going to have to work on the RFP response all alone, without Kenny, who'd been writing all the RFPs up to that point. He knew the product better than anybody, and Noah needed that knowledge to write a winning proposal response. Nobody would admit it, but the company felt like it was in limbo.

Noah left work one evening and found Brittney sitting in the driver's seat of her car in the parking lot. She was parked right next to his Jetta. Noah initially thought that she was waiting for someone, probably Ian. The two often left together after work to grab a drink. But on this day, she was only waiting for him.

"What's up, girl? What are you doing out here?" said Noah.

"I was just taking a breather before heading home. This place is a mess. How 'bout you? Off to your girlfriend?" she said in a sarcastic tone.

"I didn't know that was so upsetting to you," replied Noah.

"Well, I mean, why do all the good ones need to be taken?" replied Brittney. "Come here, sit down. Let's talk for a bit."

Noah knew that it was a bad situation, but the devil got the best of him. He put his computer in his car and sat in the passenger seat of Brittney's SUV.

"Nice car," said Noah as he absorbed the new car smell while Brittney stared at him with slutty eyes.

"I feel like we haven't gotten enough time to talk. I know things have been crazy around here. But do you like it?" asked Brittney.

"Yeah, I like it. I keep learning something new every day."

"You know, I really want you here. I know we aren't spending too much time working on the RFP, but I still appreciate your presence at this company," said Brittney.

"That's really nice of you to say. I mean, I'm also upset because I thought we would be spending time together, off regular hours. At least, that's what you said," said Noah.

"Do you mean for work? Or do you mean something else?" replied Brittney, looking to get an indication of how Noah felt.

"I mean, I'll take any opportunity I get to be close to you," said Noah, who was becoming lost in her deep blue eyes.

"Shut up, shut your fucking mouth. You're so fucking sexy. Kiss me," she said in a dominant fashion. Brittney could no longer contain her impulses.

Noah and Brittney shared an intense stare for three seconds before they leaned heads and engaged in an aggressive, sloppy kiss. He quickly slipped his hand under her skirt and started to rub on her clitoris through her silk underwear. It was hot, moist, and musty after a long day of work. The passion in that SUV was intense.

Brittney sunk into her seat and spread her legs to give Noah clearer access to her pussy. He moved her panties to the side and started to penetrate her hairy vagina aggressively with two fingers. It released loud squirts as she orgasmed onto his hand. All the while, she was rubbing his package through his pants. Brittney then unstrapped his belt and unzipped his pants to pull out his penis. She grasped it with her hands and started to jerk. After a few pumps, she leaned into his ear and whispered, "Fuck me."

But Noah had no intentions of doing that. He just wanted to establish some type of dominance over his supposed boss. To him, she smelled of cigarette smoke and was too old and too loose for his liking.

"That's not going to happen," he said to her displeasure.

"What? What do you mean? No, fuck me, right now," said Brittney, who was winded from coming so much.

"Na, that's okay. I gotta go," said Noah as he pulled his fingers out of her.

Noah stepped out of the car and adjusted his shirt as Brittney stared at him in disbelief.

"Hey, get the fuck back in here and finish what you started," demanded Brittney. "What, are you pussying out because you have a girlfriend?"

"Yeah, you stink like shit. My girlfriend doesn't," replied Noah. He got into his car and drove away as Brittney yelled obscenities at him.

"You're a fucking son-of-a-bitch! You're going to be so fucking sorry for playing with me! Say goodbye to that office I was going to assign you. I hope you enjoy your cubicle!" yelled Brittney.

Noah laughed all the way home. He wasn't exactly sure why he hooked up with Brittney. He'd never cheated on Victoria up until that point nor doubted their relationship. He knew in his heart that they were destined to be together. But Noah's life before Victoria knew few boundaries. He'd longed to feel the fire that used to burn in his soul, the same fire that once led him on the greatest adventure of his life, one complete with danger, revelation, and love. And now, he'd fallen into CannaTron's aura of corruption.

Chapter 6
The Impending Wars

The morning traffic from Dade County to Fort Lauderdale was a horrendous derby, a compassionless free-for-all where human life received no respect. For five-and-a-half months since he started working at CannaTron, Noah endured the chaos of fifty thousand Dade Countians convening on Interstate-95 for the morning commute. What separated Dade County's traffic from that of Los Angeles, Atlanta, and New York, was an overwhelming majority of Hispanics. And just like one would see in any Latin-American country, the people carried their anger, stress, and pride to the road, only leading to disorder and danger.

Noah always took the express lane to avoid congestion. It was expensive but better than being stuck in bumper-to-bumper traffic jams. Still, that decision presented its own set of problems. He dealt with maniacs who tailgated and cut off other cars at speeds above ninety miles an hour. There were early morning races between Maserati and Ferraris, Subarus and BMWs. And there were always imminent fights between hot- head gorillas and apes. One time, Noah drove past two men who pulled onto the emergency lane to exchange punches.

Noah almost got into an accident at least once a week, causing his blood pressure to elevate permanently. He would arrive to work bearing the tension, stress, and negative energy from the forty-mile commute. No matter the time he left, there was almost always an accident that stalled traffic, making it difficult to consistently get to work at eight a.m. sharp.

The worst thing about it, the one thing that bothered him more than the danger, more than the stress, and more than the assholes, was dealing with Brittney as she smoked a breakfast cigarette at the building's entrance. After their hook-up fiasco, she made it a point to stand at that same spot every morning until Noah arrived at work. Sometimes she was there with Ian. Sometimes she was there with Debbie. Other times, she was with Aziz. But the common denominator was always her. And she always had a comment for Noah if he was late.

"Why are you late?", "You're always late!", "Late Again!", "This is a problem!"

In Noah's mind, Brittney had a lot more things to worry about than him being five minutes late, especially when everyone else dictated their own schedules. He saw her friends like Ian, Jamie, and Helen get away with anything they wanted. He knew that her ball-busting was retaliation for not fucking her. Still, he swallowed his pride every morning and dealt with her attitude. But his patience was certainly being tested, and he wouldn't tolerate the double standard for too long.

The paper remained his focus. Physically, he was at work every day. But mentally, he was in research mode. Fortunately for him, the cannabis industry surrounded him with the information he needed to provide the medical world with a review of the most recent scientific data available on marijuana. The data was out there. He just wanted to compile and compress it.

Noah's entire paper was based on the endocannabinoid system, a series of cell receptors found in every major system of the body that worked to maintain the body's internal environment. These systems include the nervous system, the vascular system, and the skeletal muscle system. He explained that the human body created chemicals known as cannabinoids which either activated or deactivated endocannabinoid receptors, altering many biochemical and physiological processes in the body. Noah wanted to highlight that marijuana contained cannabinoids that bind to the same receptors to provide many medicinal benefits.

Noah researched the works of Dr. Raphael Mechoulam, a biochemist from Israel and the Godfather of marijuana. He was the first scientist to isolate the active cannabinoids of marijuana, THC (tetrahydrocannabinol), and CBD (cannabidiol). In 1964, Mechoulam found that THC was the psychoactive component of marijuana which was later found to have medicinal effects for pain, nausea, and hunger. The other component, CBD, the non-psychoactive component, was discovered to have more profound effects on the body's nervous system, vascular system, and skeletal muscle system.

The paper was broken down into a discussion of the different systems of the body, ailments related to those systems, and the results of THC and CBD treatment research trials on those ailments. He summarized studies that concluded the effects of CBD on Multiple Sclerosis, that the component modulated the CB-1 receptors in the nervous system, which reduced neurodegeneration. He also wrote about studies that concluded CBD's role as an anti-inflammatory agent in blood vessels, as a remarkable treatment for epilepsy, and as an active component that stimulated the production of the enzyme lysyl hydroxylase in bone cells, improving the rate of bone fracture healing.

The vibe at CannaTron had only gotten worse with each passing day. Aziz was on edge due to the sales team's poor performance and the plummeting sales numbers. Jamie was always hungover, calling in sick or not calling at all. Mitch had transitioned into a full-time marketing role, virtually taking himself out of the sales team in the process. Kristin was available but also hungover most days. All she cared about was her cigarette breaks when she was at work. And Helen was still the same; a loud, rude, and defiant beast.

The prank wars had become a personal vendetta for both participants, turning Zack and Bryan's friendship into a bitter rivalry. To Zack's credit, he toilet-papered Bryan's office, bombarded him with wet wads while he was on the toilet, and took off all the keys from his keyboard. Bryan, on the other hand, stole Zack's motorcycle, tin-foiled his entire office, and put mustard on his door handle and office supplies. The keyboard and mustard incidents almost led to fights, but the water balloon assault would be the tipping point.

That morning, Noah entered work through the back doors, soaking wet from head to toe. He was welcomed by the sound of Elaine and Helen having a conversation about their favorite sex positions. Neither sexagenarian was shy about their active, post-menopause sex life.

"I was up until two in the morning trying to get that thing to spit. Herb took two Viagra, and I just couldn't keep up. My arm got so tired. I just went to bed, and I think he jerked it," said Elaine.

"Oh, Viagra? Na, Carlos doesn't take that shit. He has it up all the time. When I wake up when I get home from work. I tell ya, that old man was born to fuck. He once had me bent over the grill for two hours in the backyard. It wasn't hot or anything. But finally, I told him, jackoff whenever you want. Don't be ashamed. You need to get off, and I can't always help ya," said Helen.

They heard Noah rustling items at his desk, and Elaine peeked her head around the cubicle to confirm he was there. She looked back at Helen and whispered, "Oh my God, he heard everything."

Helen was street tough. She decided to confront the situation directly. She also sensed that Noah wouldn't have a problem with the content of the conversation. She'd been watching him for quite some time.

"Hey, babe, you weren't bothered by what we said, were you?" asked Helen, who then walked over to talk to Noah.

"Na, don't worry about me. I'm not sensitive," replied Noah, who was good-natured about the conversation upon which he stumbled.

"Yeah, I could tell. You know, my husband, he's a Puerto Rican. He's a really cool guy. You know, he's a man's man. That's why I married a Latin guy like you, 'cause I like real men. Not like some of the people here," said Helen.

"Like who?" asked Noah to instigate.

"Like this one here," she said while pointing at Mitch's desk. "I mean, you see me having problems with Aziz, but this one, right here, he's no man. He's a fucking pussy. They used to have him doing sales, but he sucked. So, they moved him to marketing. Now all he does is bitch and complain about me, 'Oh, Helen is so loud. Oh, Helen yells at the customers.' But I tell ya, Albert ain't never getting rid of me. I was the first one here. When he lost everything, and this company was going down, I was the only one here. So, fuck these guys. But you, you're cool. I can tell a real man when I see one. I like that," ranted Helen.

Bryan entered the office earlier than usual with a different type of energy. He was focused, serious, and on a mission. It was his turn to retaliate against Zack for the keyboard incident. Noah, still getting over the awkwardness of the old women's conversation, noticed that Bryan was carrying a duffle bag and a bag of deflated balloons.

"Got a minute?" he said to Noah while showing him the balloons.

"Let's go," replied Noah.

They gathered in the bathroom, where Bryan used a funnel to fill the balloons with orange juice. Noah collected them as they were filled and placed them in the duffel bag.

"I'm not going to let that piece of shit get the last laugh. While he's eating his pussy-ass salad, I'm going to fly in there like a kamikaze," said Bryan.

"He's going to get pissed," said Noah.

"Fuck that guy. He's selfish and has no conscience," replied Bryan.

When they got back to the office, Aziz and Helen were fighting once again. Helen flung a stack of papers on the floor and walked out of Aziz's office. She sat at her desk and tried to continue working, but all she did was speak profanities under her breath while randomly moving items around.

"Who the fuck does this guy think he is? I don't need this shit. I swear, if I leave this place, these guys will burn. You just wait; they're all gonna burn, fucking assholes, fucking Taliban mother-fucker. This is my country, not his."

Like always, Noah just stayed quiet but found everything to be hysterical. Helen knew that he could hear. She knew that he always heard, but she didn't care. That's just who she was, shameless. Aziz's door opened, and he stepped out of the office to go have a cigarette and vent his frustrations. He was enraged. To Noah, it looked like he was on the verge of firing Helen.

Just as the door closed behind Aziz, Noah received an email from Albert. It was sent to everyone in the company. The e-mail read,

I need to know who is charging to the company credit card ending in 9494. Message me immediately!

Albert

Not a minute after that, signs of Kenny appeared for the first time in nearly a month. He replied to the email by saying,

Albert, I'm calling you right now.

Kenny's emergence sent shockwaves throughout the company. Not even Brittney, his assistant, had heard from him.

Unknown to anyone, Kenny disappeared to Spain after the E-Greens trial. He'd felt immense pressure leading up to the day of his testimony and had a mental breakdown immediately after it ended. An intense anxiety attack put him in the hospital for two days. Upon being discharged, his wife, Angela Cho, who met Kenny when he was managing a dispensary in Colorado, convinced him to fly away to heal and ponder his future. Because he'd also been absent, Albert had no idea that the company had been running without its CEO.

Charlie, who worked in the room known as the onboarding hub, was making his morning rounds with Debbie and Jamie, verifying that customers were billed for support hours. He walked by the cubicle area, joyful as usual, and noticed Mitch's absence.

"Hey, Noah, where is he? Still in Colorado?"

"I think so. Hey, come by around one. Bryan's going to attack Zack with water balloons," replied Noah.

"Where? Here? Today?" replied Charlie, interested and humored.

"Yup," said Noah.

"When are these kids gonna learn?" giggled Charlie.

"Did you see Kenny's e-mail?" asked Noah.

"Yeah, that conversation was weird," replied Charlie.

"Where the fuck have these guys been?" asked Noah.

"I don't know where Kenny has been. But Albert's been home, chilling, not giving a fuck. The old man is losing it. I mean, his mind is already gone. Do you know that he was diagnosed with early onset Alzheimer's a couple of months back?"

"Really? No, I didn't know," replied Noah.

"Yeah, Albert's a mess. This has all gotten too big for him to handle. Five years ago, when things were still new, he was on top of everything. Now, he doesn't even show his face."

Just then, Aziz returned from his cigarette break. He didn't look anybody in the eyes, walked straight into his office, and sat at his desk.

"Helen, can I see you in my office, please?" he said aloud. Helen was scared that she was going to get fired. She knew her faults. She knew that Aziz would be completely justified if he did. That was why she walked into his office with her purse in hand.

"This fucking place is crumbling. I gotta go. I'll try to get back for the show," said Charlie before leaving.

Moments later, Jerry Levine walked through the door wearing an oversized, faded, tie-dye shirt, ripped jeans, and sandals. His hair and his beard were longer than ever.

"Morning, Noah. Hey, I wrote an article and a blog post. I was wondering if you could look it over and check for spelling or grammar mistakes."

"No problem. If you want, I can post it on the website. We need all the content we can get," said Noah.

"Thanks, I'll send it over in a minute. Where the fuck is everyone?" asked Jerry.

"Aziz is yelling at Helen in his office. Mitch is in Colorado. Jamie and Kristin are both out. The bosses are still gone. Zack and Bryan are in their offices," replied Noah.

"This place is a fucking joke. Run away as soon as you can, my friend," said Jerry.

Two hours later, Zack stepped out of his office to grab lunch on time, as expected. On his way out of the office, he walked behind Noah and slapped him on the back of the head. Noah flinched forward and immediately let Zack know never to touch him again.

"If you ever fucking do that again, I'm putting you to sleep."

Zack could tell that Noah wasn't joking. But he didn't act out of malice. To him, because he was as immature as a child, it was all in good fun.

"Whoa, relax, Rodriguez. It was a joke."

"I don't give a fuck. Do that again and see what happens," said Noah to ensure that his point was understood.

Zack rolled his eyes and walked out of the office. That was when Bryan proceeded to prepare his attack. When the coast was clear, he placed and concealed his bag of orange juice balloons in a spot next to Zack's office behind the old desk that nobody used. He went back to his office to change into his sneakers and wait for Zack to return.

An hour later, CannaTron's Investment Director sat at his desk to enjoy a gourmet lunch from the Italian store across the street. As usual, he was absent-minded about the prank war and only focused on stuffing his face. He opened the styrofoam box and inhaled the delicious smell of eggplant parmesan with a Cesar salad. He wrapped a napkin underneath his collar and proceeded to bask in the joy of lunch. He forked his food and prepared to put it in his mouth. That was when Bryan appeared without warning and started to throw the balloons at Zack, soaking everything in sight with orange juice, including the food.

"What the fuck, Miller!? I thought we were done!?" yelled Zack while crouching behind his desk. His entire wardrobe got wet; his fitted shirt, his pressed slacks, and even his black leather shoes.

"Eat shit, Stansbury. Now we're even," said Bryan while continuing his attack.

"You ruined my lunch! You ruined my fucking eggplant parm!

I'm sick of this shit!" yelled Zack.

He jumped from behind his desk, charged Bryan at full force, and they started fighting. At first, it was a wrestling match. Zack took Bryan to the ground, but Bryan was much stronger and quickly got back to his feet. He charged Zack, and they both ran into Mitch's cubicle, causing the entire structure, including Noah's desk, to collapse.

Aziz stepped out of his office, and everyone ran to the scene, including Jerry, Charlie, Brittney, and Helen. Bryan and Zack wrestled on top of the destruction, exchanging body and face punches. After everyone got their entertainment's worth, Noah grabbed Bryan, and Charlie grabbed Zack. As they were being separated, Bryan kicked Zack in the testicles, marking the end of the fight. Zack fell to his knees, and Bryan left the office.

Chapter 7
The Stock Meeting

For Noah and Victoria, there was no better source of positive, natural energy than the beach. It was a place to escape the daily routine of life. They brought their mobile devices and their weed, losing all sense of time on that beach. For hours, they would smoke, relax, talk, meditate, sleep, and recharge their souls.

"So, how's the RFP going?" asked Victoria as she peeled a mandarin.

"Uh, I've done all I can do up to this point. But nobody else is doing their part. Kenny came back, but he hasn't even mentioned the RFP. He just locks himself in his office doing God-knows-what. There's some bullshit stock meeting on Monday. I guess I'll have to see him after it," said Noah, who was drinking a cold beer.

"What's the stock meeting about?" asked Victoria.

"It's about the unvalued stock that Albert promised everyone. It's all Mitch talks about. He really believes that Albert is going to make all his dreams come true. It's pathetic," said Noah.

"That's sad. The old man is fucking with these people's lives. From what you've told me, I think he's looking to sell the company and lay everyone off," said Victoria, the MBA student who was attending a group chat on her mobile device.

"I think you're right. That guy is a con artist. He pays the workers meager salaries and promises them the world. I mean, I'm almost certain that I get paid a lot more than most of the people there. Kenny tries to be some kind of leader by being all articulate and using the word 'team' way too fucking much, but he's a bitch. I can see right through that guy. Albert made him CEO to be a scapegoat for all the bullshit and pending lawsuits in that place. Every day I hear something new about his past, how he was a player in that pill-mill scandal and that he went to prison for a while for some other shit."

"Well, don't get stressed. You're only there for a little bit. Let's just enjoy the weekend and this beautiful beach," said Victoria. But it was too late. Noah couldn't get his mind off the topic.

"What pisses me off is the way guys like Aziz and Mitch conduct business. They act like hot shit at the trade shows, thinking they're special 'cause they wear suits, trying to be thugs at the same time. Meanwhile, Mitch is always stalking E-Greens on social media and trying to conjure some plan to fuck with them at the shows. They're not really liked in the industry, at least, that's what I hear."

The morning of the stock meeting, Noah encountered one of the worst sets of traffic that he'd ever seen. It had rained all night and all morning. The wet roads were the cause of multiple accidents. The line of traffic started before he even got to the highway. The on-ramp was congested with impatient drivers who wanted to forcefully create a second lane. It took him an hour to get to the express lane, where the traffic finally cleared.

The express lane and the rest of the highway were separated by a barrier of bendable poles. The only highway patrol was supposed to pass through the barrier. But in Dade County, every time that traffic was stuck, there were always assholes who recklessly zoomed onto the express lane, putting other drivers in danger.

The express lane consisted of two lanes, the left lane for faster drivers and the right lane for slower drivers. On that day, Noah felt that he was making good time in the slower lane, despite knowing he was going to be late. He wasn't going to risk his life over a job, especially for a company like CannaTron.

He was a mile from the Golden Glades Interchange when a red Camaro illegally moved through the barrier and into his lane. There was less than a second to react, or he would get killed.

"Oh, fuck!" was all he could say.

He swerved to the left lane before immediately swerving back to the right to avoid crashing into a speeding truck. His tires lost control on the wet road, but he gripped the wheel with all his strength in hopes of controlling his destiny. The front of his car knocked into the barrier poles and slid for two hundred feet. Noah maintained control of the wheel and pulled the emergency break, causing the car to finally stop. There was only a second to assess what had just happened. After confirming that he was unharmed, Noah made the sign of the cross, put the car's transmission into drive, and continued driving.

Noah arrived to work shaken and distraught, but he wasn't one to pronounce his emotions. He put on his shades and walked to the building, trying to brush off all tension before entering the office. As always, Brittney was there having a morning smoke. And, as always, she had a little comment to say.

"Here we go, late again. I can't tell you anymore; you need to call me if you're even going to be one minute late. Do you understand!? Is it sinking in!?"

Brittney's words certainly sunk deep into his head, but they didn't trigger the response she was expecting. Noah had to use every ounce of his mental strength to refrain from exploding verbally at Brittney. But he could no longer allow her to think that she was his superior. He would never accept it and chose to be passive-aggressive.

Noah stopped, gave a deep breath, looked at her, and said calmly, "Yeah, sure, whatever."

Brittney was shocked by his disrespectful attitude. She always expected the employees to fear her, fear her power, and her relationship with the executives. She made the mistake of thinking that Noah would quiver like the rest.

"Hey! Who do you think you are? Get back here!" said Brittney as Noah completely ignored her while walking into the elevator.

She marched into the office through the back doors, furious beyond measure. Noah hadn't set up his computer because he knew they weren't finished. He knew what he'd started and welcomed the confrontation with open arms.

"Noah, can we please see you in Brittney's office," said Aziz in a calm tone.

"No problem," replied Noah.

He followed them and closed the door once everyone got into the office. Brittney sat behind her desk while Aziz stood behind her. Noah sat in a chair, not knowing how he was about to react to Brittney's squawking. He wasn't afraid of getting fired, but he also knew that he was about to put himself in that position.

"Hey, I'm not following you around this place. I don't have time for that shit. You can't keep coming here at whatever time you want," said Brittney.

"Whatever time I want?" replied Noah with an intense look on his face. "Let me ask you something. Why the fuck are you so preoccupied with the time I get here? Half of the workers in this company are never here or are taking a cigarette break every hour, including you! And you know damn well that I'm not the only one who comes in late. I, at least, keep it between eight and eight-thirty. Some people stroll in right before lunch, and they never get bitched at."

Brittney was instantly intimidated by Noah's tone. But his confidence and machismo only made him seem more attractive. Still, she sought to maintain control because Aziz, her superior, was present.

"You need to worry about yourself and nobody else. This is the last time I tell you..."

That was the moment when Noah lost his shit. He could no longer sit back and be polite, not when his own integrity was being challenged. Brittney had to be put in her place, and he was happy to be the person to do it.

"Fuck you, Brittney!" yelled Noah as he stood up from his chair. The tech support team heard the yelling and quietly applauded. "I don't need to listen to your bullshit ultimatum! I mean, did you even go to college? What the fuck do you even do here? I do a good job, so you need to stop fucking with me! Other than coming in a few minutes late because I have to drive from fucking Miami, you don't have anything else on me. Because I don't kiss your ass or fuck you, you've kept me at that crumbling cubicle while a bunch of clowns sit in the offices! From there, I've witnessed more bullshit than any employee should ever have to tolerate at any respectable company," yelled Noah.

"Noah, please, calm down, man. We're not here to attack you. Obviously, you have some issues that you need to work out with Brittney. But other than that, we're just asking you to get here at eight, that's all," said Aziz while Brittney sunk into her chair to hide behind her computer monitors.

"Aziz, I can't promise that. I need a grace period of fifteen minutes. I mean, I'm a full-time employee. I'm not a contractor. That traffic is unpredictable as shit. I almost died today, and I'm not going to kill myself for anyone."

Noah left Brittney's office feeling a sense of relief, but he was still on edge. He walked through the communal area and noticed one of Bryan's gourmet sandwiches heating in the toaster oven. He was on a mental power trip and didn't want the feeling to end. So, he took the sandwich out of the oven and ate it in three bites without anybody seeing it. It was a strange impulse because he liked Bryan. But he knew that Bryan would blame Zack. At a company where everyone did or said whatever they wanted, the writer decided to manipulate the script in their little quarrel.

Noah went back to his desk and waited for the consequences of his actions to unfold. The toaster bell chimed, and he heard Bryan walk from his office to the communal area. Seconds later, he heard, "What the fuck? Where's my food?"

Bryan searched for his sandwich, but it was gone. There was no sign of it anywhere. He proceeded to walk around the office to see if someone else was eating it. He went to Brittney's office, the tech-support room, Debbie's office, the sales area, and finally, to Noah.

"What happened, man?" asked Noah.

"I left a sandwich in the toaster, and now it's gone."

"What? How? Sandwiches don't walk away," replied Noah.

"Yeah, no shit. I think fucktard over here is still playing games," said Bryan.

"Who? Zack?"

"Who else?" said Bryan.

Just then, Zack walked out of his office and stood in the doorway with his arms crossed while staring at Bryan. He was still angry about the kick to his balls and welcomed another confrontation.

"Do you have something to say?" asked Zack. "I heard my name."

"Yeah, why the fuck did you eat my sandwich? I'm done playing your stupid games, Zack," said Bryan.

"Fuck you! I didn't eat your stupid sandwich," replied Zack as he approached Bryan and got in his face.

"You're lucky, man. Real lucky," said Bryan. "I'm going to find out it was you, and if you continue to pull shit like this, I'm taking you out, trust me," said Bryan before heading back to his office.

"This fucking guy is crazy," said Zack to Noah. "I don't have time for this, Bryan. I've got more important shit to do, like making sure this company has capital and you still have a job next year."

Later that day, all the employees of CannaTron convened in the conference room for the big stock meeting. Everyone was there; Eugene, David, Bryan, Larry, Helen, Brodi, Charlie, Mitch, Aziz, Debbie, Kristin, Ian, and the minions of the support team.

The only people missing from the meeting were Jamie, Albert, and AJ. Jamie wasn't there because she was never there. Albert and AJ, the executive owners of the company, had no excuse for missing the meeting, especially one pertaining to company stock incentives.

Kenny and Brittney walked into the conference room, marking the start of the session. Noah noticed that Brittney was still pissed about the morning argument. He could see the scowl on her face as she handed everyone a presentation package. Once she was finished, Kenny stood at the front of the conference room with a PowerPoint presentation displayed on the large screen.

"Thank you, everyone, for coming. This meeting is to explain the stock incentive program that we have worked so hard to implement. But it's here. It's finally all here, ready for you and your future wealth," said Kenny before elaborating on the key bullet points. "The first thing I want to discuss what this means for you. We are making sure that your hard work doesn't go in vain." He then presented an equation that intimidated some of the workers.

$$[(X\# \text{ of shares}) \times (Y \text{ cents per share}) = (\text{Your earnings})]$$

There were no mathematicians in that room. Other than a handful of people, nobody else was prepared to absorb such a complex topic as a stock investment. But they trusted Kenny. They saw him as their leader, somebody who looked out for their best interest. So, they gave him their full attention and believed everything he said.

"This employee package includes options to acquire X number of shares at Y cents per share. Each of you will receive a personal offering in a letter that will lay out the exact option that we, Albert and I, have chosen. Your stock options are subject to a four-year vesting plan."

Kenny noticed the confused looks on most of their faces. It was part of his plan to lock them into the dream before twisting their minds with technical information that they didn't understand.

"What does this mean?" he asked everybody. "The first year that you are here, you will not be eligible for any stock options. This is known as a cliff year. After your first year at this company, you will have the right to exercise twenty-five percent of your plan. Every year after that, you will have the right to exercise an additional twenty-five percent. After five years of employment, you will have the right to exercise all your stock options. In the event that the company is acquired by a larger company, your options will remain intact, and you will be compensated for every share that you own, making you rich beyond your wildest dreams," explained Kenny with professional enthusiasm.

Without warning, Brittney's emotions had a drastic change. She went from being completely pissed to elated with greed.

"Whooooooo! Yes! Yes!" she yelled. Nobody expected the overdramatic, odd celebration.

Helen was the most confused about everything Kenny said. She raised her hand like a school-child and held it up until he called her name.

"Helen, yes, you have a question?"

"Hey, Kenny, yeah, I got a question. I need you to explain all this stuff again because I don't get it. I know I'm a bit dumb, and I don't want to waste anyone's time, but I just want to know how I get my money," said Helen as the others exchanged stares, giggled, or rolled their eyes.

"What exactly don't you get?" asked Kenny.

"All of it. I'm sorry, I'm not as smart as some of these other guys, but I need to go home and tell my husband everything that you said. And right now, none of it makes sense to me."

"No, Helen, it's okay. Let me explain. We are going to give you a certain number of shares at a very, very low price. If this company is bought by another company and we go public, the prices of those shares will increase, let's say to twenty dollars per share. But you will get to buy your shares at the price that we're giving you," said Kenny.

"So, no matter how much the price goes up, my price doesn't go up, and that's how I make more money. Okay, I get that. And who is buying the company?" asked Helen as everyone else sighed.

"Helen, stop asking so many questions. Nobody is buying the company. This is just a plan that you are being given in case the company is sold," said Brittney in a patronizing tone.

"Okay, but I still don't know how much I'm getting..." said Helen before Jerry spoke. As dumb as Helen was, she was certainly asking the right questions.

"Yeah, I have a question. Excuse me, Helen. Will our personal options be based on the current market rate for our position?"

"Yes, your options will be based on your job function and seniority. There are other factors that are involved, including the current number of employees and our current location," replied Kenny.

Zack, who had a background in finance, was the next to ask a question.

"Hey, Kenny, what happens to my vested shares if I leave the company before my entire vesting schedule is complete?"

"Good question, Zack. In the event that you leave on your own free will, you will get to keep anything vested as long as you exercise your options within ninety days of leaving the company. The company does have the right to buy back your exercised shares if you leave before the liquidity period," replied Kenny.

"Thank you," replied Zack.

"Are there any other questions?" asked Kenny. But nobody answered.

Despite the confusion, there was a shared sense of enthusiasm among the workers. Noah returned to his cubicle and found Mitch glowing with joy. He was leaning back in his chair with his arms folded behind his head, exposing his armpit stains. He stared at the ceiling like a boy in love, daydreaming of his fortune.

"Aahhh, I can taste the millions," said Mitch as Noah walked by.

"Yeah, I bet you can," replied Noah, who had no interest in hearing Kenny's bullshit.

"You don't seem too excited about becoming a millionaire before the age of forty. Hell, I know Brodi is excited to become a millionaire," said Mitch to Brodi, who was returning to his office.

"Fuck yeah, I'm ready. I mean, I've already won the lottery once, but another million won't hurt," replied Brodi.

"Wait, what do you mean? Are you serious?" asked Noah.

"Mitch?" said Brodi.

"Dipshit over here got some winning numbers and got paid 25,000 a year for the rest of his life."

"No shit," replied Noah. "Technically, you never have to work again."

"True, but I love working for Albert. I've been with him for almost ten years, running his medical clinics. But I'd rather be here, working in the cannabis industry."

The only person who didn't seem to be in a good mood after the meeting was Zack. He was locked in his office, playing the role of a loan shark. The others could hear him screaming at a borrower who was holding out on his pay. For not being a tough guy, Zack certainly played the role well when it came to money.

"I'm done chasing you! I gave you the loan; now pay the fuck up! Do you hear me!? Pay the fuck up! I don't care what problems you have! Get me my fucking moneyyyyyy!"

"What the fuck is wrong with him?" asked Noah. "Who knows? I heard he's on thin ice with Albert because he hasn't brought any capital investors to the company," said Mitch.

The door opened, and Zack came out of his office, snarling like a gorilla. He didn't talk to anybody. He just exited the office, slamming the door on his way out. They could hear him yelling at himself while waiting for the elevator.

"Fuck this fucking guy! Fuck him!"

Bryan returned to the back area and found the others conversing by Mitch's desk. He approached Brodi and showed him an e-mail that he had received from the office of the governor of Louisiana. Both Bryan and Brodi wanted to be Robert's right-hand man and often sought to one-up each other. Brodi felt that he had seniority over Bryan because he'd worked for Albert for so long. But Bryan didn't care about Brodi's sense of entitlement. He had a law degree, whereas Brodi had nothing.

"Check this out. Get a good look at it," flaunted Bryan. "From the office of Governor Jindal."

"Oh, so you took my lead about Louisiana legalizing and reached out to them behind my back? Good job," said Brodi with a look of disgust on his face. He took a deep puff from his vape pen and blew the smoke into the air.

"Is that all that you have to say? You never even knew about that website until I showed it to you a week before I wrote this e-mail," said Bryan.

"Man, whatever, leave me alone. I have a Pre-Algebra exam tonight, and I gotta finish studying these notecards," said the uneducated thirty-something-year-old who enjoyed the luxury of his own office.

"Where do you go to school?" asked Noah out of curiosity.

"DeVry," replied Brodi.

"Huh, wow, enjoy your office," replied Noah with thick sarcasm.

Zack left the premises and went to his nearby apartment to get high and take a power nap. He returned to the office refreshed and with a new-found urgency to find the company new capital partners. He followed up on some leads, but nobody answered. So, he left the same message four times in a row.

"This is Zack Stansbury; I'm reaching out to you to discuss a life-altering opportunity with CannaTron. We are the leading cannabis tracking software company with secured government contracts in Oregon and New York. I would love to sit down with you and discuss a remarkable investment opportunity with our company."

He felt helpless and alone. Zack was responsible for bringing CannaTron, its first capital investor, outside of the board members. Ivory Capital invested $250,000 in certified company stock. It was a big deal at the time, but Zack hadn't been able to secure another deal since. He knew that his job was on the line and needed to think of a way to bring Albert more money. While he pondered his next move at his desk, Brittney stepped into his office. She was feeling angry and vulnerable and wanted attention from somebody, anybody.

"God, Zack, that shirt fits your body really well. Have you been working out?" asked Brittney while standing at his doorway.

"Always, babe. I'm glad you noticed," replied Zack.

"How can't I? You're hot," replied Brittney in a typical, aggressive, slutty tone.

Zack and Brodi's offices were next to each other, and Brittney made it a point to flirt with both men to try and make Noah jealous. She wanted him to know that she was desired by others.

"So, what time are we going out tonight, Brodi?" she asked as Noah walked back to his desk with a hot cup of coffee.

"I didn't know we had plans," replied Brodi while sitting at his desk, reviewing his note cards.

"Yeah, you, me, Zack, and Mitch; right, Mitch?" said Brittney, purposefully leaving Noah out of the conversation as though he gave a shit.

Noah sat there with a grin across his face. He could feel Brittney's coldness with every word that came out of her mouth. But he wasn't bothered. He'd scolded her and got away with it. For the remainder of his time at CannaTron, Noah knew that Brittney would never bother him again. He found it hilarious when Zack and Brittney walked out of the office together to fuck in his BMW.

Chapter 8
Cleaning House

The stock meeting invigorated company morale. One week later, Albert and Kenny hired a new Chief Financial Officer, Eduardo Rios, and a new Chief Data Scientist, Alonzo Iverson, to take CannaTron to the next level of success. The executives wanted to inject the company with industry professionals who had substantial education and experience. The system's flaws were exposed, and financial records were in shambles. If the company was going to survive, the bosses needed to make the capital investment required to deliver an optimal product.

Kenny waited until two weeks before the Washington RFP was due to start involving himself in the development process. His role was to review all of Noah's final responses after they'd been reviewed by Ian and edited a second time. During that final stretch, Noah and Ian spent long hours working on the RFP in the conference room. They worked well together. Every time Noah was finished editing a technical requirements response, Ian, who almost had a degree in Information Technology, would review the response before sending it off to Kenny.

Noah knew they had differences, but there was also mutual respect. It wasn't until the fourth day they worked together that things got awkward. That was when Noah received further insight into the relationship between Ian and Albert.

They were both working independently on their computers when Albert casually walked into the conference room. He was leaving for the day, wearing his expensive shades, a suit, and diamond earrings. As usual, he was holding his spastic poodle.

"Hey, guys, how's it going?" asked Albert.

"Great, Albert, how are you?" replied Noah.

"Good, thanks for asking," said Albert before he looked at Ian. "Uh, Ian, I want to go to Key West this weekend."

"Okay, I guess you're feeling better. I'll find a room. Who else is going?" asked Ian.

"Just us, two nights," replied Albert.

"Ooh, that should be nice. But I thought you were throwing Guinevere another doggy party this weekend. Like with jet skis, DJs, and liquor."

"No, her partying days are over. Besides, she likes Duvall Street," said Albert while looking at Guinevere, the poodle.

"Okay, I'll bring the bathing suit you got me. It's cute," said Ian with that famous twinkle in his eye.

"Ah, don't worry about it. We won't need them," joked Albert with a grin on his face.

Noah wasn't surprised by what he was witnessing, especially not after the conversation he witnessed between Ian and Mark Smith. But it was confirmed to him that Ian was Albert's boy toy and not just his personal secretary. Such distractions should have daunted his focus, but he was able to deliver a polished proposal without delay.

Meanwhile, the sales team was still struggling to reach the monthly quota. And the customer support team was being marked throughout the industry as incompetent and incapable. After multiple server outages that Eugene was unable to prevent, hundreds of commercial customers in Oregon were unhappy with the system. That resulted in E-Greens stealing fifteen to twenty customers a week. To make things worse, the state government was threatening to void CannaTron's contract.

One afternoon, Aziz was in his office reviewing the quarterly sales reports from Jamie, Kristen, and Helen. He looked at each figure with intensity, trying to pinpoint his strongest and weakest markets. It didn't take long for him to find inconsistencies in Helen's work. As always, her updated numbers and activities didn't match the final reported numbers. For Aziz, it wasn't a minor occurrence. It was the last excuse that he needed to get rid of Helen, once and for all.

"Helen, can you get in here?" said Aziz from his office.

Helen was caught off guard while focusing on her social media feed.

"Huh? What? Okay," she replied before walking into Aziz's office.

"Helen, your numbers are off again. You haven't made any of the numbers that you created at the beginning of the month again. That's a serious problem. I know you have a pipeline, but your disregard for professionalism has caused you to continually fall short on your monthly sales. That being said, I've made the decision to release you from the company," announced Aziz.

"Are you fucking serious!? You know what!? Fuck you, Aziz! I'm tired of your shit! Albert's never going to fire me. We're pals. I was here before you, before blondie, before Mitch, before anybody," replied Helen.

"You're insane if you think I'm going to let you go behind my back and involve Albert. This is my decision. Get your shit and get out of here," replied Aziz.

"You're really firing me? C'mon, Aziz. I know we have problems, but you can't fire me. I've got bills to pay, and Brittney said the company is giving out insurance next month," pleaded Helen as her eyes started to water.

"I'm sorry. My decision is final. Leave your key card and go," was all Aziz had left to say.

Helen was frozen from shock. It took her a minute to comprehend what was happening. Without saying another word, she turned around and walked out of Aziz's office in tears. She put the key card on the desk, grabbed her things, and left CannaTron before anybody else, other than Noah, could see her crying. And just like that, crazy Helen's days at CannaTron were over. It came swiftly and without a show.

Helen wouldn't be the last person to leave that month. A week later, Eugene was fired for server outages in Oregon. The incident cost the company a lot of money, more than Albert Abraham could ever tolerate losing.

David confiscated Eugene's computer and soon discovered a humiliating secret. Everybody knew that Eugene was gay, but David found out that he was also a freak of the night. While cleaning out old computer files, he found a folder that was titled "Late Night Fun." In that folder were more than 100 video recordings of Eugene dancing naked in the office during night shifts. Sometimes he was in costume, partially naked, wearing things like Zorro masks, luchador masks, or bunny ears. Other times, he was completely nude.

The third person to get fired that month was the lawyer Jerry Levine. Other than the executives, nobody knew why Jerry was fired. That day, he just walked into his office and grabbed some personal belongings. He left the office when he was done, but not without giving Noah, Mitch, and Bryan a final piece of advice.

"Fellas, keep fighting the good fight. Remember, nobody owns you, especially not Babylon; Jah bless," he said. Noah didn't know if the firing had anything to do with the blog post that Jerry wrote. After reading it over and making some corrections, he simply posted it on the company's website. The title, "The Death of Ethics in Big Business," should have been an indicator of the trouble to come.

All of this occurred within the first two weeks that the new CFO, Eduardo Rios, was hired. He was struggling to assimilate himself into the company's culture. Until his arrival, Cannatron's financials were overlooked by Debbie, which left the company's balance sheet in disarray. The amount of work that he had to do to fix the company was immense and presumably impossible.

Nothing made sense to him. There was no cash flow. After deals were closed, implementation processes took twice as long and cost twice as much to complete. Along with bills, payroll, and the expensive renovations that he made to the office, Albert's company was running on a negative cash flow. He was funding it with his own fortune.

Eduardo wasn't shy when explaining this to Aziz and Kenny. He told them that hundreds of transactions hadn't been accounted for over the years. Assets and liabilities were never categorized correctly, the bookkeeping system was never taken seriously, and budgets were never properly allocated. All the while, Aziz and

Kenny gave the Yale graduated CPA a smug attitude as though he had no option but to fix the problem.

During those two weeks of corporate restructuring, the only thing to run smoothly was the proposal process. Because of Noah's and Ian's contributions, Kenny was able to finish his final review and send the entire proposal package to Washington before the deadline. In a time when people were getting fired, Noah felt that he'd done enough to secure his job until he found a better one.

The day after he submitted the proposal, Kenny called Noah into his office. As always, he looked exhausted and frail. He was also going through a bronchial infection that had him coughing aggressively and spitting out mucus. But among all the chaos, he became aware that Noah was the least of his worries. At CannaTron, a capable and autonomous employee with no emotional or social baggage was a rarity. Kenny understood this and wanted to make amends.

"Noah, thank you for coming here. I'm going to keep this short and sweet. Uh, I know that I was absent a lot for the last month. Still, your efforts haven't gone unnoticed. While, at times, it seemed like things were falling apart, I felt relief knowing that the RFP was in good hands," said Kenny.

"You know, I really wasn't sure what the hell was going on the entire time. I just focused on my part and hoped it would be enough. I'm glad I could help."

Kenny wasn't sure how to take Noah's response. To him, it sounded like Noah was complaining. He wasn't used to any of the workers talking to him on an even level, probably because he purposefully surrounded himself with people of lesser intelligence.

Still, he wasn't going to create tension by confronting a valued employee about it. Instead, he looked to reward Noah.

"So, how do you feel about Puerto Rico? The government is broke, and they've recently established a cannabis program, hoping that it could... stimulate the economy. I've been going back and forth recently, trying to get us in with the governor. I need someone to visit Goldwin Laboratories. They're the biggest grower in San Juan. You want to go?"

"That would be a great experience. Yes, I'd love to go," replied Noah.

"Great, you'll also be accompanying Zack to the Ganja Business Show. Just be present, describe the software, look around, and answer questions. Everything that you need to know is in the RFP, so I'm sure you're fully prepared. Uh, with regards to Zack, keep an eye on him. Sometimes he tends to speak on matters that he shouldn't. And he always looks to party in the evenings. Don't get caught up in his bullshit. I prefer you not to smell like liquor when conducting business," said Kenny.

"No worries, but thanks. I've wanted to go to a grow since I got here. I won't let you down," said Noah.

Two days later, Noah found himself shit-faced at an airport with Zack Stansbury. From the moment they met at the airport bar, they started to pour away Bloody Marys and Vodka Tonics. They drank for almost two hours until an announcement was made that their plane was boarding. Noah and Zack eventually paid their bill, stumbled through the terminal, and boarded the plane drunk.

Zack continued to party while Noah tried to relax. The stewardess served the first round of drinks thirty minutes after take-off. Zack started with a beer before switching to whiskey. As soon as the coast was clear, he took out an Adderall pill, crushed it, and snorted it on the flight table. Noah was numbed to the debauchery and could only laugh at Zack's pathetic cry for attention. Snorting pills was the Florida way, but he'd never seen the necessity of putting unnatural drugs in his body.

The couple sitting across from them saw everything. They were disgusted and appalled by Zack but opted to ignore the degenerate. Zack gave a demented laugh while leaning his head back as the bitter drip made its way down his throat. Then he looked at Noah with his over-stimulated but dead eyes.

"Do you want some, Rodriguez?" asked Zack, who didn't want to be the only douche-bag on the plane.

"No," slurred Noah in a resentful tone. "Keep your white-devil poison away from me."

"You know, you're a mystery, Rodriguez. Why don't you want my drugs? It's an offering. One should never reject an offering," replied Zack.

"'Cause I'm not like you. I'm loved. And stop looking at me with those creepy eyes."

Zack just laughed, stared at Noah with his creepy eyes, and then ordered another drink.

"Yes, waitress, uno más, por favor."

Noah eventually fell asleep while Zack continued to drink the entire way to San Juan. They got off the airplane and located their belongings at the baggage claim. From there, they got into a taxi and headed to the hotel. Along the way, Noah noticed and admired the fertile land, the crumbling conditions, and the legal cock fighting arenas.

After checking into their rooms, Noah and Zack met in the lobby to go out for dinner. Both men got some rest and cleaned up for the night. Considering how belligerent Zack had gotten, Noah was shocked to see him functioning at a normal level. Other than being a bit groggy, he was able to project himself in a sober fashion.

"Bro, I don't remember shit about the plane ride. I'm pretty sure I tried to fuck the stewardess on my way to the bathroom," said Zack.

"So, where are we going?" asked Noah.

"To find some pussy," said Zack before he put on his party shades and went to find a taxi. "Follow me."

The two co-workers were taken to Old San Juan, where they ate dinner at a steak house and continued binge drinking with Bacardi and cokes. They went bar hopping after dinner and finally settled at a festive salsa lounge. Three hours later, Noah found himself sitting at the bar while Zack showed off his dance moves to the local women. Despite being an alcoholic and a drug addict, Noah saw Zack as a talented and bright individual, confident and vocal. He always admired those extroverted qualities in any person because it was the complete opposite of who he was.

Zack eventually decided to rejoin Noah at the bar and express his contentment with the evening. He found Noah in the middle of a spirited debate with the bartender and some locals about who was the better boxer of his era, Oscar De La Hoya, or the Puerto Rican champion, Felix "Tito" Trinidad. He knew the topic would spark a conversation down in Old San Juan.

"Oscar dominated that fight for eight rounds, and you all know it. I love Tito, but he lost that fight to a better boxer, plain and simple."

"¿¡Que!? ¿¡Que!? Este Americano está loco," said the bartender, who was entertained by the conversation. "Por tener los huevos para decir eso en San Juan, I'll give you a fucking shot on the house." Noah couldn't pass up the offer. He downed the tequila like a champ, no salt, no lime.

"Noah," slurred Zack as he sat on one of the stools. "I don't know what the fuck you're doing here instead of dancing with some of these Puerto Rican chicks."

"Dude, I'm getting married in May. I'm having a good time watching you have a good time. I'm good," replied Noah.

"Ah, marriage. It's a good thing to be married. I was once married to a doctor. I put her through medical school, and she got rid of me just like that," confessed Zack as he snapped his fingers.

"What did you do? Fuck around?" asked Noah.

"Yup, I fucked around a lot, too much," he slurred while staring deeply into the thought of her. "But hey, I'm thirty-five. I'm sitting on a boatload of money and a piece of Albert's company. And I got pussy right here waiting for me and my new friend, Noah," said Zack. He finished his rum and coke, leaving only the ice, and turned his attention to the women who were giggling his way. "I'm gonna go dance a little more," he said.

"Alright, I think I'll take a cab back to the hotel. We have to be at Goldwin Laboratories in seven hours. You sure you'd rather not come back with me?" said Noah.

"No, fuck that. I'll be back there in an hour with one of these chicks, if not both of them," said Zack. Noah paid his bar tab and hopped into a taxi. On the way to the hotel, he noticed a text message from Kenny that read:

[Zack hasn't picked up his phone. I assume he's out somewhere getting drunk. If that's the case, go to Goldwin Labs by yourself tomorrow. I don't want him embarrassing the company or himself].

It became apparent to Noah that Kenny knew Zack well. He didn't wake up in time the next morning to meet in the lobby. Noah waited for as long as he could, but the taxi's meter was running. He had no choice but to leave at the scheduled time and go to the laboratory by himself.

The taxi drove to a remote location in the mountains which were dense with forest and greenery. The 4- cylinder cab struggled at times to make the sharp turns around the narrow roads that traveled steeply up the mountains. They eventually came to a security gate, where an armed guard approached the car. Noah rolled down his window and said, "Hello, my name is Noah Rodriguez. I'm here from CannaTron. I have a meeting with Ms. Beatriz Buelvas."

He took Noah's identification and reviewed the guest list. After his credentials were confirmed, the gate opened, and the taxi drove onto the property. It was a well-funded laboratory with ample space and multiple facilities.

The car arrived at the entrance. Noah thanked the taxi driver, paid him, and reported to the central office. He entered the facility and filled out an entry form and a waiver. From there, he proceeded to the prep room, where he put protective wear over his clothes to adhere to the lab's regulations. That was where he met the tour guide, Beatriz Buelvas. She was a young Ph.D. candidate who quickly caught his attention through her physical and intellectual attributions.

"Hello, my name is Beatriz Buelvas. I will be your tour guide today." She had a captivating smile, wide eyes, and long, dark hair. But her accent was the sexiest of all.

"Hello, Noah Rodriguez; nice to meet you," he said before shaking her hand.

They passed to the security room, where Noah left his items, including his wallet, watch, and cell phone, in a locker. From there, they walked through a set of large double doors before being overwhelmed by the sight of five thousand marijuana plants in a climate-controlled facility.

"Welcome to cannabis land," said Beatriz as Noah forgot for a moment how to breathe.

"Excuse me for being overwhelmed, but this is awesome," said Noah.

Beatriz smiled and replied, "Don't worry, I've seen a guy almost feint before. You're fine. It's beautiful, isn't it?"

"It sure is," replied Noah. "It's the most beautiful thing I've ever seen."

Noah gazed deeply into the trees to get a glimpse of all the different buds. He absorbed all the colors and textures of earthly goodness. The odors from the terpenes lured him in every direction.

"The earliest seeds were genetically modified, and the clones were grown with a specific purpose," explained Beatriz while walking alongside Noah, who was speechless. "These are the Indicas; over there is the Sativas, and those in the middle are all Hybrids. Each strain has its own medicinal value. Some plants were grown to help hunger; other plants were grown to treat conditions such as Chron's disease."

They walked to a particular tree with dense buds surrounding the stems. "This strain is a hybrid Kush. It's given to chemotherapy patients to help them with nausea and pain." She picked a bud, smelled it, and put it in front of Noah's face. "This is OG Kush; it's one of my favorite strains. Notice the piney, earthy aroma."

Next, they walked by a glass-plated room that was isolated from the rest of the grow. It was a storage location that held the final yields of hundreds of plants. The buds were stored in large, polymer trash bags and mounted in piles onto a wheeling cart. There were twenty full bags per wheeling cart and fifteen wheeling-carts in the room.

"And this is why we need your help. These buds were grown for neurodegenerative treatment research. They will be distributed to our processing and packaging center before final delivery to the clinics. We are under intense pressure from the government to track every gram. But we've had complications along the way with our inventory system. We need a system that's specific for this type of industry."

"That's a lot of cannabis to track. But our software can certainly help you with that. It's fully integrated with solutions to help every step of the growth, cultivation, processing, storage, and transportation of legal cannabis."

Noah walked with an analytical mind through the rest of the facility; the grow, the drying rooms, the harvest rooms, and the processing centers. He was enchanted by the entire facility and Beatriz, too, up until the end of the tour. That was the moment she chose to take a cured marijuana bud and pack it into a glass pipe.

"Noah, we want to ensure that only the freshest cannabis leaves this plant. This bud is of the highest quality. Would you like to try and tell me what you think?" she said.

"Gladly," said Noah before grabbing the unused glass pipe and taking the best hit of weed that he'd ever taken in his life.

He got back to the hotel after the tour and walked straight to Zack's room to see if he was okay. He knocked three times before somebody answered the door. It was one of the girls Zack met at the bar. She was fully naked, and so was Zack, who was still in bed with another girl.

"Hey, Zack, you coming to the show?" said Noah while standing at the doorway.

"Uh, what? Who is that, Rodriguez?" moaned Zack.

"Yeah, man. The show starts in three hours, and we have to be there to set up," replied Noah.

"Yeah, dude. Let me clean up and say goodbye to, uh, what's your name?" he said while looking at the naked Puerto Rican woman.

Zack kept his word and cleaned up well for the show. Both men looked sharp in their dark suits and slicked hair. But that couldn't hide the fact that CannaTron, like all the other companies there, was still small-time. Their booth was a disaster. It lacked clean branding quality, and the graphics display was loud and cluttered with content and software images. It was Mitch's prized achievement, and it was garbage. Still, Noah and Zack did their best to show a strong front for the company.

The event had a large turnout, but it became obvious to Noah how primitive the industry was. There were cannabis businesses of all kinds offering a wide range of services like t-shirt printing, cloud services, marketing services, compliance training, and legal counsel. There were also pipe and glassworks vendors who were looking to establish partnerships with larger companies.

The majority of those vendors were hippies trying to tap into the market before it boomed like a gold rush. They didn't know it yet, but their chance of success was extremely low. In general, the average lifespan of a business in the cannabis industry was six months. Most projects were self-funded or funded by investment capitalists. There was certainly no financial backing from the banks. In the marijuana industry, for the most part, the only businesses that generated capital were the ones involved in the plant's production and supply chain; the growers, the processors, the vendors, and a handful of tech companies.

Noah and Zack stood in front of vendor lot 23, handing out reading material and marketing to anyone who spoke with them. The Puerto Rican marijuana market was still new, so their main goal was to establish a presence among the citizens and potential retail customers. Their presence at that event was crucial in their quest to corner the market. Once CannaTron won the Puerto Rico Health Department's monitoring contract, the licensees would be forced by the government to purchase and use the software.

After answering questions all morning, Zack was approached by a reporter from Dope Business Magazine, a well-established publication in the cannabis industry. For Zack, it was the perfect moment to put CannaTron in the spotlight and attract investors. He needed that opportunity to revive his career and save his job. He fixed his collar and buttoned his suit as she introduced herself.

"Hello, Cannatron. I'm Vicky Byrne with Dope Business Magazine. I was wondering if you had a second to talk about CannaTron's recent success. I mean, with two state contracts under your belt, I can only wonder how much the company will grow in the next few years."

The woman interviewing him was a tall blonde with an enchanting smile. Zack couldn't help but stare her deeply in the eyes throughout the interview, among other places on her body. His mind fell under a spell. Then he started getting images in his head of the two women that he'd slept with the previous evening. Suddenly, his thoughts were jolted, and his focus was completely disrupted.

"Vicky, I would be honored to be interviewed by someone so beautiful. My name is Zack Stansbury, and I'm the Investment Director at CannaTron," said Zack, suave and articulate.

"Well, Zack, CannaTron has certainly built momentum in the last year after winning the New York and Oregon contracts. To what do you owe your success?" asked Vicky.

"Our success is a derivative of many factors, including our work ethic, our commitment to our customers, and our vast knowledge of compliance and regulation in the cannabis industry," replied Zack.

"The competitive pool is growing for tech companies. How do you plan to stay ahead of the competition?" asked Vicky.

"It's simple, Vicky. We set the bar. We are the only cannabis tracking solution in the entire industry. We've crushed our opponents along the way and left them in peril. Currently, CannaTron is twice as big as E- Greens, and, on average, we are taking twenty customers from them per month. But they will soon meet their demise because they're violating federal law by paying off government officials in states waiting to legalize cannabis medically and/or recreationally."

Noah couldn't believe what he'd heard. Zack had opened his mouth publicly about CannaTron's competitor in the middle of litigation. Soon, his words would be blasted all over the internet.

They returned home the next day. It was a Friday. Zack continued to party after the show and went home to sleep off his hangover. Noah also didn't go to work that day. But his absence was excused. He and Victoria moved north to Boynton Beach to a pristine condo on the Intracoastal Waterway. They used the day to move their items and transfer the pets.

"This is a great place to start our marriage, baby. Good job finding it," said Victoria while unpacking utensils in the modern kitchen with stainless steel appliances.

"I'm glad you're happy, my love," said Noah while putting down a heavy box. This place is closer to work, and the traffic heading south isn't anywhere near as bad as the Miami traffic," said Noah.

He looked around the apartment and admired the layout. Then he walked out to the wrap-around balcony to view the entire city of Boynton Beach all the way out west to the Arthur Marshall Everglades Reserve. From that viewpoint, he saw a flat bed of treetops that traversed as far up north as he could see. Victoria followed him to the balcony and wrapped her arms around his waist.

"Look at that view. I've never seen anything like it," said Victoria. "You know, I just want to tell you that I'm happy with whatever you decide to do. I know you're under a lot of pressure to get the research paper published, and this job really isn't the best place to work. But whatever you decide to do after the paper is done, I'll support it."

Noah turned to Victoria and gave her a loving kiss on the lips before saying, "Thank you, my love. You're the reason we've gotten this far, and you're the reason we'll get as far as we do." They stared out to the horizon and observed all the details that comprised the view. It was a small reward for their daily efforts.

Chapter 9
The Consequences

There were no more cannabis conventions, shows, or events for the rest of the year, which meant that Mitch would be in the office every day for the next three months. That also meant that Noah would have to endure his whiney rants daily. It's not that Noah didn't like Mitch, nor did Mitch give two-flying-fucks about Noah's opinion, but it was clear to Noah that Mitch couldn't be trusted. And yet, it wasn't hard for them to cohabitate the area and work in peace.

"So, how was the show?" asked Mitch while staring at his computer screen.

"Good. It was small, a lot of pretenders," replied Noah.

"Who did you meet?" asked Mitch.

"Some of the licensees, a doctor that's been doing extensive research on pot for more than ten years. Dr. Altah was his name," said Noah.

"Oh, I met that guy in Oregon. I know who he is. He's got long hair, wears sandals, little Arab guy," replied Mitch.

"Yeah, that's him."

"He slipped me some nuggets at a show in Boston," said Mitch.

"Isn't that risky? I mean, how do you know it isn't a cop or the feds?" asked Noah.

"I don't know. I didn't ask him for anything. He just mentioned that he wanted me to try his stuff. So, I just glanced at my bag, and he put it in there. I smoked it in Kenny's hotel room with Aziz."

"Did Kenny smoke?" asked Noah.

"Yeah, he took some hits," replied Mitch.

"I also had the pleasure of spending quality time with Zack," added Noah.

"Oh, shit, I was afraid of this. What did he do?" asked Mitch as he finally turned to look at Noah.

"We got fucked up the first night. I went back to the room early, but he stayed up all night with some girls he had met. He didn't make it to the lab the next morning, but he cleaned up for the show," revealed Noah.

"He didn't go to the grow with you?" asked Mitch.

"Nope, but he made up for it at the show. He spoke to a lot of people, some magazine writers and potential investors."

"What Magazine? Bud Wave?"

"No, Dope Business," replied Noah. "Some gorgeous woman interviewed him."

"Who? That Vicky chick?" confirmed Mitch.

"Yeah, Vicky Byrne," said Noah.

"What did he say?"

"I'm not sure," replied Noah. He didn't squeal on Zack. Instead, he wanted to see how things unraveled.

That question would be answered later in the afternoon after

Dope Business published an article about the event. The first one to see it was Charlie while at his desk. Other than being an implementation specialist, he was also CannaTron's internet troll. Every day, he scanned the internet for articles about CannaTron and their competitors to keep the bosses up to date. No news pertaining to CannaTron got past him, and it didn't take long to find Vicky Byrne's article on the Dope Business website.

"Oh fuck, Zack, you're finished," said Charlie after reading the headline.

[CANNATRON CRUSHING THE COMPETITORS, SAYS INVESTMENT DIRECTOR]

The first thing that Charlie did was e-mail the link to Mitch, who would reaffirm the criticalness of the situation. After that, he immediately walked over to Mitch's desk to discuss.

"Hey, what do you think?" asked Charlie.

"I think Zack's going to get fired. We have to show this to Aziz right now," said Mitch. "The longer this is out there, the more likely someone we don't want to read this will. Is this what you were talking about, Noah?"

Noah looked at the headline and confirmed the writer, Vicky Byrne.

"Yup, that's it. Is he even here?" asked Noah.

"Who? Zack? No, he hasn't come in since you guys got back," replied Mitch. "But this shit has to come down, now."

Mitch forwarded the link to Aziz, who was in a meeting with Kenny and Albert. He saw the e-mail on his phone and immediately stood up to leave and address the issue.

"Excuse me, Albert. I need to talk to my sales team," he said before leaving the room. He walked to the back area to get an explanation from Mitch.

"What the fuck is this? Noah, did Zack really say this in Puerto Rico?" asked Aziz.

"I'm afraid so. I couldn't stop him. He just said it, and the reporter recorded everything," replied Noah.

"Fuck! Fuck! Fuck! Fuck!" said Aziz. "Where is he?"

"None of us have seen him," said Mitch.

Aziz immediately took out his phone and called Zack, but there was no answer. After hearing the beep, he hung up the phone and called a second time. Again, there was no answer. That caused him to grow more and more furious by the second. He paced back and forth behind Noah and Mitch's cubicles like a thug, ready for retaliation. His only option was to leave a stern voicemail message.

"Zack, you need to call me immediately. This is Aziz."

Aziz hung up the phone and took a second to regain his composer. He could feel his blood pressure rising as the seconds passed without getting a call back from Zack.

"Let me know as soon as you see Zack come into the office. For now, we need to get that article down. Mitch, call Dope Magazine and tell them to take it off their site and social media. Have you guys even checked if they posted it to their social media pages?" asked Aziz.

"Fuck, it says here that it's been shared more than five hundred times," said Mitch.

"Call them up and get it down, now! I gotta go tell Kenny and Albert about this," said Aziz before leaving the room.

Zack didn't show up to work for the rest of the day. He went on a drug binge as soon as he got home from the airport and hadn't stopped partying since, continuing his downward spiral into an abyss of misery. He went to K.O.D. and spent all of Monday paying strippers for coke and sex. He eventually passed out at the strip club while receiving his third blow job of the day. The bouncers threw him in a cab and gave the driver his license.

The front-desk attendant at his building had to help him up the elevator and into his apartment. Zack woke up on Tuesday to find thirty missed calls, fifteen voice messages, and twenty text messages from Aziz, Albert, and Kenny.

Everybody else at the office was well aware of the situation, and the company was in damage control. Kenny wrote an apology script and gave it to the tech support team to read to all their customers. Albert contacted E-Greens' CEO in Colorado to assure her that the content in the article wasn't true.

In good faith, Dope Business Magazine kept the article posted but added a comment from Kenny that discredited Zack's comments.

"...I would like to assure you that these are not the opinions of CannaTron, and Mr. Stansbury spoke at his own discretion..."

To further add to CannaTron's turmoil that Tuesday, The Washington State Liquor and Cannabis Board abruptly chose E-Greens for their cannabis tracking system. Kenny was the first to receive the e-mail and immediately started to panic. As thoughts of failure and dishevelment spun inside his head, he pounded his fists on the desk and cried like a baby.

"Why is this happening to me?" he released in frustration.

After nearly having a full-blown panic attack, he tried to regain his composure. He took a drink of water and proceeded to write a company-wide e-mail to announce the decision while crying.

Team, this morning, I received notification from WSLCB that E-Greens won the Washington state monitoring contract. I know this news is upsetting to all of you, especially to those who worked so diligently on this RFP. But this loss does not reflect our team or our work ethic, and we will certainly file a request to review the records and see exactly why the state did not choose our system. That being said, I challenge all of you to take this loss as a learning experience. We will overcome and become stronger because of this. Only in the face of defeat do we find out who we are.

Sincerely,

Kenny Cho

CEO CannaTron

After reading the e-mail, Noah opened the attachment that was included. It was a copy of the final RFP response that was sent from CannaTron to the state. To his disappointment, he discovered that his work had not been used. In the end, the CEO decided to cut and paste the content from his old proposals instead of using Noah's work. And as he expected, it was poorly written.

"Fuck that guy, can't write for shit," said Noah to himself.

From there on, all that mattered was his research paper. CannaTron's future, Kenny's vision, their promises of wealth, none of it meant anything to him. He was going to finish his paper on their dollar and get out as soon as he could. Since his cubicle had the vantage point of monitoring everyone that entered and exited the office, he worked freely on his paper throughout the day without worrying about getting caught. If anybody approached his desk, he would minimize the windows and proceed as though he was working on a blog or a manual.

With regard to the events in Puerto Rico, Noah wasn't sure if he was going to get reprimanded. In his mind, somebody had to get blamed, and if Zack wasn't around, he thought he was next in line. He kept to himself while everyone else scrambled in the chaos. All the while, Zack was conjuring the guts to go to work and face his fate.

Noah was in the communal area filling a cup of coffee when he heard Zack's voice. He walked to the back area to see if Zack was aware of what was happening. To his amusement, among all the things that Zack had pending to discuss at the office, he and Bryan were arguing over the missing sandwich.

"I can't fucking believe that you're coming to me with this shit! Fuck you, get out of my face!" yelled Zack.

"Just be a man and admit it. I know you took it. You know you took it. I want you to apologize for your actions," replied Bryan.

"Why do you care so much about a fucking sandwich?" said Zack as he and Bryan stood face to face.

"I'm a man of principle. It's about the principle, Zack. Just admit that you stole my sandwich, and I'll go about my way," said Bryan.

Noah thought that he was about to see a second fight between Zack and Bryan until Kenny walked into the room.

"Zack, Noah, I need to see you in the conference room," he said.

The executives and board members were waiting for Zack and Noah. They sat around the table in a frenzy while assessing the situation. Around the conference table sat Albert Abraham, AJ Lauria, Robert Peterson, and Kenny Cho. Zack and Noah sat down while Albert and AJ reviewed the article from Dope Business Magazine. Kenny didn't waste time confronting the issue.

"Zack, can you explain what in God's name you were thinking when you spoke to Ms. Vicky Byrne?"

"Yeah, first of all, I just want to say that Noah..."

Noah instantly made a defensive face after hearing his name. *What the fuck are you mentioning my name for?* He thought.

"Noah? This has nothing to do with Noah. Did you see this article? The headline says you. The words came from you. Again, what did you think when you said this?" said Albert.

"I was trying to establish our dominant presence in the industry. I wanted to attract more investors. Vicky Byrne was highlighting our growth, and I felt a need, to be honest about our success," replied Zack.

"And by highlighting our success, you also put a claim that we're taking customers from E-Greens," said Kenny.

"Yeah, fuck those guys. We need to put them in their place. I don't see the problem with this," said Zack.

"You don't see the problem with making an inaccurate statement about our competitor who is currently suing us for slander and false advertisement, among other things?" said Kenny.

AJ, the co-owner of the company, didn't say a word. Not even at a board meeting did he feel inclined to speak. Robert Peterson just sat there with his arms crossed, also not saying a word. It seemed as though they had nothing left to add to the conversation like their minds had already been made.

"This has nothing to do with the lawsuit," said Zack before Albert violently intervened.

"You, stupid son-of-a-bitch, this has everything to do with that lawsuit! And from the intel that we've gathered today, the Washington board based their final decision on your stupid comments. Don't you think it's a coincidence that the day I read this article, I got an e-mail from Washington saying that E-Greens won the RFP?"

Zack was speechless. He knew that he was moments away from getting fired. But there was nothing that he could say. To him, it was simple math. He cost the company a five-million-dollar contract, and that was grounds for immediate dismissal.

"My next question is for you, Noah," said Kenny. "We aren't putting any blame on you for Zack's comments. But in your own words, can you confirm what Zack was doing the night before?"

Noah was put in a difficult position. The executives wanted him to rat on somebody who was in the room. He looked at Zack, who was obviously concerned. But Noah knew that he needed to ensure the survival of his goals.

"We went out for some drinks. I left early; Zack stayed until late."

"And did Zack go with you to Goldwin Laboratories the following morning?" asked Kenny.

"No, he didn't," replied Noah.

"Why not?" asked Kenny.

"Because he was hung over. He got too fucked up and couldn't wake up for our meeting," said Noah.

That was all the confirmation the executives needed to hear. They were tired of Zack's antics. He'd failed at doing his job and never lived up to Albert's expectations. He was also a clown, and everybody knew it. The fact that his comments were directly correlated to the Washington RFP loss was unforgivable. Kenny, AJ, Albert, and Robert Peterson all looked at each other to confirm their final decision.

"Zack, I want to thank you for your time here at CannaTron. But I feel that your recent actions put us in a very difficult situation. I'm sorry, but we're letting you go, effective immediately. Go grab your things and vacate the premises within the hour," said Albert.

"No, no, no, you don't want to do this, Albert. I have a huge list of investors that have been blowing up my phone, looking for a sit-down meeting with you."

The executives didn't care about his plea, not even as Zack started crying. It was a pathetic display of weakness that made everyone else feel uncomfortable. Zack wouldn't be getting any sympathy from that crowd.

"C'mon, Kenny. I thought we were cool. You can't fire me. I love this company," pleaded Zack one final time.

"I'm sorry, Zack. The decision is final," replied Kenny.

"AJ, after I loaned you one hundred thousand dollars, you're still going to fire me? Hell, you exchanged company stock for that loan," said Zack.

"The board will decide on that matter. For now, you must go," said AJ.

Neither Kenny, Albert, nor Robert knew anything about a transaction of stock between Zack and AJ. They were shocked at the revelation. It was another disaster that needed to be addressed.

By the end of the day, Zack had gathered his belongings and left the office. Noah decided to leave home after the meeting as well. He was enraged with Albert and Kenny for involving him in Zack's firing. He was also pissed about everything that happened with the proposal, whether it affected the outcome or not. He got home and spent the rest of the evening in the gym, taking out his frustrations with every rep he lifted.

Chapter 10
Babylon Falling

It was winter in Florida, and CannaTron was experiencing the consequences of its abrupt increase in employee turnover. After Helen was fired, Jamie and Kristin were the only members left of the sales team. They bore the pressure of achieving the monthly sales quota of one hundred thousand dollars. The commission gains were now larger for them because of Helen's departure, but the pressure placed on Kenny, which he placed on Aziz, which he placed on Jamie and Kristin, only resulted in a dysfunctional organization.

"Aziz! Why the fuck aren't we looking for more help? All we need is one more person to get back to where we were," said Jamie to her boss while inside his office.

"Look, you're just going to have to do the best you can for now! We exceeded our budget last year, and Eduardo is still working on next year's budget," said Aziz.

"The best I can!? That's all you got for me!? The best I can!? I swear you don't know what the fuck you're doing!" said Jamie with her dirty, little mouth.

"Hey! Who do you think you are!? I'm a fucking doctor! You aren't shit! Either you learn some respect or get the fuck out of here!" yelled Aziz.

"You think I care that I'm fired!? Go ahead! See how you do with only one salesperson; I don't need this shit," yelled Jamie.

"Okay, fine, go ahead and test the job market. I remember how you told me all those stories of how much you loved being a cocktail waitress at a strip club. You either learn to respect me as your boss and as a professional, or get the fuck out!"

"You can't fire me. Kenny would never get rid of me. We're friends. I'll just wait until he comes back, and we'll see who gets fired!" Jamie walked out of the office, fuming with rage, and slammed the door. The force caused the sales billboard to fall to the ground.

To help deal with such insubordination, Noah purchased an oil pen from Bryan Miller and took hits of weed oil throughout the day, zoning him out while writing his paper. He took as many hits as he wanted because the marijuana oil was odorless. It was a carbon dioxide extract, high in THC and CBD, giving Noah the perfect high to write like a machine while blocking out distractions.

Kristin found herself alone for the rest of the day after Jamie went home. The silence made her uncomfortable, and she decided to find the only person who was ever around to talk. She walked to the other side of the cubicle area and lingered behind Noah before saying in a soft tone, "God, it's so quiet here."

Noah took notice, turned around, and replied, "Hey, Kristin, what's going on?"

"Not much, I just don't like the quiet. It makes me uncomfortable. How are you?" she said as she leaned against Mitch's desk. As usual, she wasn't wearing a bra, exposing her perky breasts as she stuck her chest out to further get Noah's attention. Kristin was in heat.

"Yeah, I don't know what the fuck is going on with this place.

Other than that, I'm good… writing," said Noah.

"I've sensed bad energy in the office lately. Do you know what I mean? Like, everybody is just crazy right now. Do you believe in meditation?" asked Kristin.

"Yeah, I do. Why?" replied Noah.

"I think we need to do some more meditation at work. There's too much bad energy. I feel like we all need to have like a group session to fix things up and help to lighten the mood."

"Do you really believe that?" asked Noah.

"Well, my dad was a veteran who died of cancer. But while he was sick, like, after the chemo, we would smoke all the time and meditate. He used to be an angry person, but the meditation helped him cope with his illness and actually made him a nicer person. His soul was cleansed before he died."

Noah tried listening to what she was saying, but her breasts were too distracting. The white tang top left little for the imagination. She caught him staring twice at her areolas but said nothing.

"I'm sorry to hear about your dad. But maybe we do need to meditate more in this place, work out the bad vibes like you said," said Noah.

"Then it's settled. Watch; I'll show you how it's done," said Kristin before taking a seat on the floor.

"Are we really doing this?" asked Noah, who also sat on the floor.

"Yep, and you'll see, you're gonna feel great," replied Kristin.

She sat with her legs crossed Indian style, closed her eyes, and took a deep breath. She placed her hands against her abdomen and started to move them toward her belly button. Noah also sat Indian style to join the fun, but he didn't close his eyes. Instead, he decided to observe Kristin as she sensually rubbed her body. Her hands moved lower with every breath she took.

"First, I want you to focus on your breathing. Focus as you inhale air into your lungs and exhale from your body. Feel your diaphragm expand as you breathe in and contract as you breathe out. Feel the cells of your body illuminate with energy with each breath of air. That is your mind awakening," said Kristin before entering into a deep breathing pattern. Noah tried participating, but he could only focus on the way Kristin was rubbing her little belly.

"Breath in the positive energy of the world. Breathe out the negative energy. Create a library in your mind of positive words that illuminate every second of your existence... You are strong. You are brave. Your life is wonderful. Breathe in... breathe out... all that you seek will be yours. There is no competition. You've already won. Now absorb the light of the world, breathe in... and breath out all which inhibits you; fear, anger, doubt, regret, stress."

Before he knew it, he saw Kristin rubbing her clitoris through her worn-out spandex pants. She held a deep breathing rhythm for five minutes while pleasuring herself in front of Noah. Her fingers circled around her genitals while her body entered an exotic trance. Her breathing became heavier as she neared her climax. All Noah could do was stare in awe as she had an orgasm right there in front of him. When it was over, Kristin opened her eyes, noticed Noah staring at her, and said, "Now, that's much better. Don't you think?"

But Noah was speechless. He just held a silly look on his face and nodded as Kristin stood. "Good talk; I'm going to have a cigarette if anybody asks," she said before walking out of the office. She left Noah sitting on the floor, unable to move because of his rock-hard boner.

"That was fucking awesome," was all he could say.

The next day proved to be a huge turning point for Albert Abraham and CannaTron. Noah showed up to work and started his day as usual with a cup of coffee. He took a minute to sit at the counter and look outside at the active world, pondering his life and its direction. All the while, he still had Kristin's exposition on his mind.

He watched the morning rush as cars drove east and west on Las Olas Boulevard, although they were supposed to be driving at slower speeds. He sipped his coffee while soothing meditation music played throughout the office. For a brief second, he became numb to any pending work responsibilities, feeling an unusual sense of peace. It seemed as though the masturbation meditation had some type of effect on him. For a moment, the day seemed as though it wouldn't be filled with any sort of drama until he heard Albert yelling from his office.

"How can he even do this!?" expressed Albert while standing over his desk. "It's not bad enough that he's suing us, but now he has to put this shit on the internet for everybody to read? Unbelievable!"

"He knows if he's within his legal rights. Who knows what other information he'll release," replied Aziz.

"I mean, what the fuck is he trying to prove? This could ruin us," said an enraged Albert. He had to grind his teeth to hold back the anger. "I told Kenny not to have the stock incentive meeting, to hold it off until the summer. It was a good idea at first, but our cash flow projections are skewed. This company can't pay off what he promised. We're fucked, I tell you. We're fucked."

"Have you heard from Kenny?" asked Aziz.

"Yeah, he called me as soon as he got my e-mail. I don't know where he is, but he said that he would be in tomorrow," said Albert in a calmer tone.

Three months earlier, Jerry Levine retaliated in an unprecedented way to his dismissal from CannaTron. He sued for a breach of contract, financial damages, and his full stock valuation. Immediately after getting fired, Jerry claimed that the company owed him the full value of his stock options because, as Kenny stated at the employee stock meeting, he had already earned twenty-five percent of it after two years of employment. He reached out to Albert and Kenny multiple times for a response through phone calls, e-mail, and text messages. But they refused to give him a stock valuation or a company valuation without any lawful excuse or justification.

During the first deposition that occurred at the Broward County courthouse, Jerry attempted to have Kenny's address and confirm CannaTron's stock value. But Cannatron's lawyer didn't allow that to happen. Jerry, who represented himself, claimed that CannaTron was committing fraud by disclosing specific details of the actual stock value, whether it was worth a fraction of a penny or fifteen dollars per share. Canna Tron's lawyers defended that none of the employees who were offered shares through a Stock Purchase Agreement were forced to purchase the shares and that the company had no financial interest in selling off its shares on the financial market. That was their excuse for not providing the full stock valuation.

In retaliation, Jerry decided to play dirty. If he was going to be denied his money, then he would make sure that Albert lost money as well. Just before he was fired, one of his final duties was to mediate a private transaction between AJ Lauria and Zack Stansbury. The deal consisted of Zack loaning AJ one hundred thousand dollars because, according to AJ, he needed the money to help his mother retire. In return, AJ satisfied his debt by transferring sixteen thousand shares of CannaTron common stock at six dollars and sixty cents per share. Zack agreed, and he deposited one hundred thousand dollars to AJ's holding company, TechVault Unlimited. The deal went undisclosed to the other board members, leaving them in disbelief when Jerry sought to purchase a portion of those shares from Zack at a newly estimated price per share.

"Zack, how are you? This is Jerry Levine," said Jerry while in Jamaica smoking ganja with a Rastafarian High Priest in Kingston Town.

"Hey, Jerry, it's good to hear from you. To what do I owe this pleasure?" said Zack, who was having dinner with a Mexican model at Y.O.L.O.

"I called to see how you were doing. I heard that you got to let go," said Jerry.

"How did you hear?" asked Zack, who thought the call was unusual.

"I read the updated article, which now says that you are no longer with the company," replied Jerry.

"Yeah, well, what's done is done. How can I help you?" said Zack.

"Zack, I'm getting straight to the point. I'd like to buy a portion of your CannaTron shares. Does that interest you?" said Jerry.

"Ufff, I mean, the money would be nice right now. But why do you want it?" asked Zack.

"Because they're refusing to give me a valuation, although I know that AJ gave you a valuation for the stock. He didn't tell anybody about the arrangement he made with you. So now, I see an opportunity to set our own valuation since you are officially a shareholder of the company. You know, they're illegally denying me my shares, and I know what they're worth. Your valuation can help that and the others at the company who have earned stock," said Jerry.

"So, how do we come to a valuation?"

"We can base it on everything we know about the company. About all the shit they talk, about all the sales and state contracts they've won, and all the media hoopla," said Jerry.

"Huh, that's actually not a bad idea. Albert's going to be pissed. This could lead to war," said Zack.

"Fuck those guys. Look, once you sell the shares to me, I'll be responsible for ownership. I pay you, you collect, sign over the shares, and the fallout comes on me."

"So, I can sell you one hundred shares. But I seriously don't know what price to sell them at," said Zack, who'd left his date to discuss the matter by the valet.

"Well, let's think, two state contracts, about twenty- five

employees, all the office supply, fifteen hundred customers, leaders in the industry, blah, blah, blah; I'd say that we can value the company at... two hundred million. You like that?"

"Alright, let's say, forty-five dollars a share; for one hundred shares, that's forty-five hundred. But you know this is all total bullshit, right?"

"Well, my friend, I'm just playing the game that they started. I'm not going anywhere until they pay me what's mine. I'll send over the paperwork, and if you need council on the matter, I'm also here to offer my legal services."

"Alright, man. Let's do this. Let me know what Albert says," said Zack before hanging up the phone.

The reason Jerry could devise such a plan was that none of the employees who'd already vested one year at CannaTron were given an explanation on the valuation of the company, hence, a valuation of their shares. That was because, unknown to them, Albert planned to sell his shares in the company before anyone realized it. He had no intention of running an IPO or taking the company public.

Albert was a serial entrepreneur and wanted to turn his profit and split as soon as possible. He needed to hold off his workers with an incentive that never existed. Kenny covered Albert's plan by establishing the stock incentive program. It was enough bullshit to keep the workers working until the sell-off was complete.

Days later, CannaTron received a correspondence from Jerry that detailed the transaction. The company retaliated immediately with a counter-lawsuit against both Jerry and Zack. They claimed that Jerry sought to purchase Zack's shares at an excessive price to either extort CannaTron or to make himself a shareholder.

Kenny, as the CEO of the company, filed a complaint of Civil Conspiracy against the two former employees. Zack had no choice but to hire Jerry to be his legal representative for the matter. But before the courts could settle on anything, the CannaTron board members held an emergency meeting with Albert's lawyer, Sam Williams.

The board was convened by its chairman, AJ Lauria. Kenny Cho was in the conference room, but Sam Williams, Robert Peterson, and Frank Delfino all attended the meeting via telephone. Albert was ill, dealing with the consequences of poorly maintaining his diabetes, and was unable to attend. Brittney joined Kenny in the conference room to record the meeting minutes.

The primary purpose of the meeting was to discuss the TechVault Unlimited/Stansbury transaction. It was in response to the e-mail that Kenny sent one week earlier to all the members of the Board of Directors informing them of the transaction. AJ knew it was time to explain the deal and hoped that Sam Williams could help him avoid it in some way.

"So, it has been discussed to me that the board is seeking to file a Right of Refusal Order with respect to the loan transaction of shares between TechVault Unlimited and Mr. Zack Stansbury," said Kenny.

"Yes, the purpose of this meeting is to have all the board members vote on whether we waive or execute our Right of First Refusal with respect to the transaction," said AJ.

"My goodness, this is such a mess, AJ. How could you withhold this information from us? What were the terms of the deal again," asked Frank Delfino, who was resting by the pool in his lavish Fort Lauderdale mansion.

"This information was sent to you last week in an e-mail on March 16th," replied Kenny.

"What e-mail? I didn't get an e-mail?" said Frank Delfino. "Do you people do anything right? I've doubted for quite some time if this was all a wise investment. I think I'd be better off selling my shares before it's too late."

While still holding his poker face, Kenny started to sweat on the back of his neck. He wasn't a shareholder and knew that he wasn't indispensable, especially when the board wasn't happy.

"Yeah, I'll attest as well; I never got that e-mail," said Sam Williams.

"It's okay. I'll explain again," said AJ. "Zack Stansbury, our former Investment Director who was fired three months ago, extended one hundred thousand dollars to my holding company, TechVault Unlimited. This was a loan that I needed to settle some debts for my mom and put a down payment on a house. I paid him back with shares of the company. The full loan value that is owed to Zack is one hundred and ten thousand dollars because of his interest charge."

"What? Wait, uh, who wants to sell the shares?" asked the befuddled Delfino.

"Again, I'm exchanging my shares for a note due on a loan that was extended from Zack to me," said AJ.

"What the fuck are you saying!? In English!" yelled Delfino.

"Zack loaned AJ the money, and AJ paid Zack back in

company shares," said Kenny.

"Oh my God! And what was the valuation of the shares?" asked Delfino.

"The valuation is exactly identical to what our capital investor, Ivory Capital, holds. It's six dollars and sixty cents per share.

"There is no way that we can have Zack as a company shareholder. It's irrational and illogical. I'm going on record saying that I want to exercise the company's Right of Refusal and keep Zack Stansbury off our capitalization table and keep the shares. This is such a mess. Kenny, how did you not see this happening?"

Kenny knew better than to reply. AJ was the culprit, but he was going to take the blame. Frank Delfino was his boss. Whatever he decided was final.

"Frank, the company valuation officially sits at twenty- three million," said Kenny.

"Then no, my decision is final. We cannot have these shares floating around in the open market," said Delfino.

"Sam, what's your opinion?" said Kenny.

"I agree with Frank. No matter what, it's a lose-lose situation for CannaTron. It's a very unfortunate and very irresponsible situation for the company to be put in. The deal should have been disclosed as soon as it happened. I can't agree with Jerry's stock valuation. Therefore, I also think it's best to execute the Right of Refusal," said Sam Williams while at his ocean-side office.

Before filing the Right of Refusal, the board members asked their Director of Government Affairs, Robert Peterson, to call Zack directly and advise him to sever ties with Jerry and withdraw from the transaction. Jerry had become a nuisance that wasn't going away. The board members wanted to see if a stern message would resonate in Zack's head.

"Zack, how are you? It's Robert," said Robert with a frank undertone.

"Good old Robert Peterson. What's up, my man?" replied Zack in good spirits while lying on his couch watching television.

"Zack, I'm going to make this short and sweet. No bullshit, are you listening?" said Robert.

"What the fuck? What's up?" replied Zack, who sat upwards.

"Look, we're cool, but this crap that's going on with Jerry, it's gotta stop. He called us asking for a stock valuation because he was purchasing your shares. Is that true?"

"Robert, thanks for calling, but I don't think we have anything to discuss. If Jerry contacted you for a stock valuation, I suggest you give it to him and everyone else that deserves it."

"I told you, cut the crap. How much are you selling your shares for?" questioned Robert.

"Well, if you really must know, based on all the shit that's talked at the company, all the media articles, and all the hype, I thought forty-five dollars per share was fair."

"You can't do that, Zack. And you know it. That's way too high. It's extortion. Your valuation was at six dollars or something like that. I told you I wasn't bullshitting. You don't know what you're getting into. If you continue, there are going to be repercussions, whether financially from court fees that you can't afford or through other means. You know Albert. You know how he handles things.

He doesn't fuck around. His friends don't fuck around. Don't make this mistake," said Robert before hanging up the phone.

Zack heard Robert Peterson's warning. He spent that evening in seclusion, smoking weed on his high-rise balcony, wondering if he was putting his life in danger. He still wanted to work in the cannabis industry and didn't want to smear his name by participating in any form of devious business. He also didn't want to jeopardize the CannaTron stock that he owned. After getting ripped out of his skull, he could no longer juggle his thoughts. Zack concluded his decision, picked up the phone, and called Jerry.

"Zack, I was just about to call you. I called CannaTron...," said Jerry.

"I'm sorry, Jerry," interrupted Zack. "I really wanted to do this, but Robert called me. He told me not to go forward with this deal. He wasn't fucking around, Jerry. It was definitely a threat. I'd never heard this tone in his voice. He sounded like a fucking gangster. I'm sorry, man. My life isn't worth it. My career isn't worth it. I can't do it."

"Wait, but did he threaten you?" asked Jerry.

"Of course, he threatened me, but that's beside the fact. I'm still young, and I don't want certain people in the industry to see me as a dishonest person."

"Zack, nobody will touch you. Albert's just trying to use his muscle. Don't back out of this deal. We need to set the bar for us and for everybody else, he's lied to. If not, we'll all get screwed."

"I'm sorry, Jerry. My mind is made up. I'm sorry," said Zack before hanging up the phone.

The next day, Jerry withdrew all representation of Zack Stansbury by filing a notice through the court. CannaTron, staying committed to Robert Peterson's threats, dismissed their Civil Conspiracy lawsuit against Jerry and Zack.

But the cannabis lawyer wasn't finished. He was still committed to his mission and was now out for blood. He knew that Albert's lawyers would avoid deposition dates to keep Albert and Kenny from testifying. So, Jerry, knowing of his legal limits, used his information to unleash a full-out assault on Albert, Kenny, and Sam Williams. He leaked damaging information online through multiple social media outlets. This included e-mail exchanges and court documents about the stock program, Kenny, board members, the litigation, and about Sam Williams. He not only wanted to get what was owed to him, but he also wanted to destroy Cannatron's reputation at the same time. In the name of Jah, he became the most annoying troll imaginable on social media. His effort in the matter was of epic proportion.

The first damaging item that Jerry leaked was a scanned copy of a Motion to Consolidate, which mapped the entire sequence of the lawsuit up to that point. It included excerpts from the deposition in which Kenny refused to give Jerry a stock valuation. The second damaging item was an e-mail exchange between Albert and Jerry in which Albert asserted that Kenny would not receive stock in the company because he didn't trust him. Kenny had always worked under the assumption that he would receive stock like he was above the others.

The third and most disturbing item that Jerry leaked was another e-mail exchange that gave details about a sexual harassment lawsuit against Albert from a former CannaTron employee, Lawrence Madison. Jerry was Albert's counsel on the matter and had every e-mail stored on a hard drive. He wanted to paint a picture of Albert that not only portrayed him as an unethical businessman but as a dangerous member of society. He hoped that it would evade other government officials from doing business with the company.

Additionally, Jerry focused on smearing Albert and Kenny's names through creative social-media posts and memes. The posts highlighted Albert's criminal history, involvement in Florida's pill-mill epidemic, two felony convictions for credit-card fraud, his failing health, and even his homosexual lifestyle.

He posted an unfavorable picture of Albert and Frank Delfino wearing extravagant, flamboyant, Versace suits while holding their matching poodles. The caption read, "CannaTron's mighty leader and his lover, Frank Delfino." Albert wasn't openly gay within the cannabis community and sought to hide his sexual orientation from government officials because he was a Republican. He was also old-school, from a different time when such matters were never discussed.

It only took a couple of hours for every employee at CannaTron to start seeing Jerry's posts. Everybody could immediately sense the severity of the situation. They were all learning, together, the harsh reality that their stock meant nothing. To those who didn't know about Albert's past, they were learning that their boss was a criminal and a convicted felon. And to those who remembered Lawrence Madison, the revelation of sexual harassment was unnerving.

Noah and Mitch were glued to their computer monitors, reading every detail of Jerry's feed. The more they scrolled, the more they learned, and the more entertaining it got. Noah found it all hilarious while Mitch was slowly starting to feel sick.

"Hey, Mitch, who's this guy, Lawrence Madison?" asked Noah, while reading Jerry's leaked material.

"I'm not exactly sure. I think it's Unicorn," replied Mitch.

"Unicorn? Why did you call him that?"

"He wore tight t-shirts with unicorns on them. He was blonde with long hair. He wore jewelry and always painted his nails. I don't think you were here when he was here. Charlie and I just called him Unicorn. I think he was an assistant to Albert," said Mitch.

The description jolted Noah's memory. He remembered Lawrence from his first day at work. He was the colorful person who was being yelled at by Albert, the one with the awkward fashion sense. That was when Noah realized that it was the first and last time that he ever saw Lawrence at the company.

"Well, this is no surprise. As far as we know, our stock is worth the value of a pencil. I don't know about you, but I saw this coming," said Noah.

"Which one are you reading?" asked Mitch.

"The e-mail about Kenny's stock," replied Noah.

The e-mail chain read:

From Jerry: *Hi Albert, when Kenny returns, I suggest that he initiates, for tax purposes, a stock incentive program for the company. With his financial background, I figured he could be useful this way. It's a big advantage for the company from a tax standpoint to implement an incentive program.*

From Albert: *What? Stock for Kenny? Are you crazy? NO STOCK FOR KENNY!*

From Jerry: *I never suggested stock for Kenny. I just suggested implementing an incentives program. It's a task he can do as CFO.*

From Albert: *I understand. I just don't want to put Kenny in a position of power. I don't trust him. I don't trust his face.*

From Jerry: *I don't want to put him in a position of power, either. But I figured he has to do something if you're paying him. Let's just have him do some research on the matter. Even though he abandoned us once before, you still need to get your money's worth.*

"What are you reading?" Noah asked Mitch.

"The deposition," said Mitch, who grew paler by the minute.

The deposition read something like this:

By Mr. Levine:

Q. Mr. Cho, did you see a Notice of Withdrawal on the document the first time you reviewed it?

A. Yes, I see a Notice of Withdrawal.

Q. When was this document sent to you?

A. This document was sent to me on September 10th, 2015.

Q. Now, just to avoid any confusion, does September 10th come before September 11th?

A. Yes, it does.

Mr. Williams: Objection. For what year?

Mr. Levine: For every year since the existence of time. By Mr. Levine:

Q. Mr. Cho, you were saying?

A. I have already answered your question. But if you don't remember for obvious reasons, then I'll repeat. Yes, September 10th comes before September 11th for every year.

Q. Thank you. Now, I'd like to go back to the letter in question.

A. Which letter?

Q. Well, if you don't remember for obvious reasons, I'll repeat it. The September 13th letter from Mr. Frank Delfino, Albert's business partner, life partner, and co-owner of CannaTron, to Mr. Williams. That's exhibit 10.

Mr. Williams: Then, can you please be clear as to what you're referencing?

Q. Mr. Cho, does the letter state that I, Jerry Levine, am seeking the monetary valuation of the stock incentives which I was promised?

A. Yes.

Q. And is that your signature at the bottom of Mr. Delfino's letter?

A. Yes, it is.

Q. So, you've been aware of my desire to obtain this information that I'm rightfully and legally owed.

A. Yes, I'm aware of the information you are trying to attain.

Q. Then, can you tell us the valuation of the stock which was offered to me on August 17th in the document labeled Stock Purchase Agreement with your signature, which is shown here on exhibit 11?

A. There was no exact valuation disclosed at that time.

Q. Do you mean there was no valuation at all?

A. Yes.

Q. Can you tell us here today, under oath, the stock valuation for shares of CannaTron?

Mr. Williams: Objection; my client has been informed by counsel not to answer that question.

Mr. Levine: This is a deposition, and your client, Mr. Cho, is under oath.

By Mr. Levine.

Q. Mr. Cho, can you tell the court the monetary valuation of one share of CannaTron stock?

Mr. Cho looks at his attorney.

Mr. Williams: Do not answer that question, Kenny.

Mr. Levine: Are you refusing, once again, to provide me with this information?

Q. Mr. Cho?

A. I...

Mr. Williams: Do not answer that question.

Jerry also posted on the events that happened after the deposition. He revealed that Sam Williams chased him down, yelling and cursing his name in the court halls. After catching his breath, he said, "I don't know who you think you are, but you better stop playing games, Jerry."

"I'm not playing games. I'm just going after what's mine," replied Jerry Levine.

"You're fucking with the wrong people. You will regret the day you messed with Albert and me. Okay? I know people. You'll see. You'll regret it," said Mr. Williams.

Just as Mitch and Noah finished reading the e-mail, they saw Eduardo Rios walk out of the office through the back doors. He had his coat in one arm and work bag in the other. Debbie followed him while saying, "Eduardo, please don't leave." He didn't reply. The door closed, and she turned to Noah with an upset look.

"Eduardo just quit. Fuck, our CFO just quit. He just dropped everything and left."

"Well, hey, I guess you've been promoted. Congratulations!" said Noah sarcastically.

Through the power of social media, Jerry Levine got his message across to the entire cannabis industry. He knew the right people to target, ultimately bringing skepticism, doubt, and shame to Albert and his entire company. Potential investors no longer wanted to do business with CannaTron. Current investors wanted answers. And the dedicated workers of CannaTron had to question the legitimacy of their stock.

Chapter 11
The Unfixable

Jerry's leaked documents put CannaTron on the brink of disaster. The turmoil grew every day as Kenny tried frantically to keep his job. Customers were calling to cancel orders, and government officials from Oregon and New York were threatening to pull out of their contracts. It was up to Kenny to preserve those relationships while Aziz dealt with customers and media outlets. Kenny called the government agencies in Hawaii, Alaska, Nevada, and New Mexico to defend the revelations. Those were states that already had some form of cannabis legalization and were in the market for a tracking system. He hoped to save face and assure the stability of the company to future customers. But some officials had already made up their minds and vowed not to do business with CannaTron in the future.

Noah paid no attention to the distractions. He was in celebratory bliss after finding out that his research paper was picked up by the Journal of Integrative Medicine. The final paper was titled *"The Current State of Medical Cannabis Research."* The editors of the journal had already viewed the material and confirmed its approval for publication. All he had left to do was to edit some of the reference citations.

One afternoon, Noah was finalizing the edits for his paper when Albert strolled into the cubicle area while talking on the phone to a government official from Nevada. It was a heated conversation, one that involved fierce profanity and malice. It started at his office and continued all the way to the back area. "The last guy that crossed me, God rest his soul, learned real quick about the mistake he made." Such comments only confirmed to Noah that Albert was nothing more than a thug with business savvy and a fortune.

"Yes, well, you don't want to do anything illegal while abusing your power because that would only make my favorite tactics fair game," said Albert while using the speakerphone.

"Do you think you have the money or force to take on the state of Nevada? We'll fuck you and take your shitty company at the same time," said Arnold Schumer, Director at the Division of Public and Behavioral Health.

"You could cost me five million dollars in court fees, and that wouldn't affect me in any way. So, bring it. I love a good fight, and I welcome it. If this is war, then be ready. I fight dirty," said Albert before hanging up the phone.

The old man took a breath to regain his energy. Unlike the days when he was a street thug brawling in Brooklyn, the adrenaline rush from confrontation now took its toll. Then he looked at Noah and said, "I'll skin them, fry them, and have them for lunch."

Albert began walking back to his office when he felt a thunderous pain overtake his livelihood. Suddenly, he clasped his chest and fell to the ground. He was having a heart attack right in front of Noah. Debbie heard the fall and ran out of her office. "Oh my God" she yelled. "Albert! Somebody call 911."

Noah hesitated before rushing to Albert's side with his cell phone. With his graduate degree in Bio-Sciences and previous CPR training, he was technically qualified to begin resuscitation. But at the last second, he opted not to help. After everything, Noah had formed his own opinion about Albert, and it wasn't a good one.

As the former felon gasped for air, Noah just scowled at his pathetic face and decided to let nature take its course. Instead, he walked downstairs to wait for the ambulance. As he exited the elevator on the first floor, he ran into Brittney, who was coming back from lunch. There was an awkward stare for a second before Noah said, Albert just had a heart attack upstairs. I came down to wait for the ambulance."

"What? Where? Oh my God!" she said as the elevator door closed. Noah strolled to the waiting area that was polluted with cigarette buds. He sat on a wall, took out his oil pen, and got high while waiting for the ambulance. He'd taken ten rips before he heard the sirens from down the street. By the time it got there, Noah was blazed out of his skull. He waved the paramedics down and pointed them to the entrance. As they ran out of the truck, he said, "6th floor, six-o-one."

Once all the paramedics went upstairs, Noah hopped off the wall and walked to his car. He felt no sorrow for Albert and thought, *He's probably getting what he deserves.* He had enough of the madness and needed to ponder his exit from the company. Noah unlocked the car, got inside, turned on the ignition, and drove away without knowing if his boss was dead or alive.

He spent that weekend at the beach with Victoria. There was no better place to focus on his next professional move. As usual, they rested on a lounge chair, smoking a blunt and watching the waves. His heavy mind drifted from thought to thought as Victoria talked about party favors for the wedding.

"I was thinking that we place the dove ornaments at each seat. They're also picture frames that say *"thank you"* on the back. What do you think, baby?"

"Huh? Sure, that sounds good," replied Noah as he stared into the depths of the ocean.

"You're not even listening," said Victoria.

"Yes, I am. The white doves sound nice."

"I know when something is on your mind. What's wrong?" asked Victoria.

"Just thinking about work. I wonder if Albert died?" said Noah while giggling.

He took a hit of the blunt and blew the smoke into the sky. He passed it to Victoria and continued, "I don't know why I just left. But I must be really sick of that place. The drive still sucks, the people are rotten, and there's no professionalism. Now that I know all this shit about Albert, why would I stay? Why would anyone stay? He fucking lied to all his employees, promising stock in the company just so nobody would quit. He's a bad guy."

"If you gotta quit now, then do it. I've got my new remote job. We'll be fine while you look for work. I don't want you to be stressed out at this place anymore. You've written your paper; now you can move on," said Victoria before taking a hit. "You don't need that place."

They walked down the beach, southbound, hoping to forget about work, the wedding, or anything else that burdened their minds. The ocean waves splashed along the shoreline as high tide started to emerge. The wind gust created a cloud of sea mist along the shore, cooling anyone it touched.

While Victoria was picking up colorful seashells for her home collection, she noticed an aggressive splash in the water about two hundred feet from shore. Noah noticed the rustling as well and got closer to the shoreline for a better look. They also saw bait fish, by the hundreds, splashing in and out of the water as though something was disrupting their migration north. Seconds later, a brown dorsal fin emerged from the water. After further analysis, Noah determined what it was.

"That's a nurse shark, baby," he said.

The eight-foot shark fed on the bait fish as the sun started to set in the west. There was nobody else around to witness the beautiful act of nature. The fin came in and out of the water each time the shark sought to trap the school of fish. After a couple of minutes, a second dorsal fin emerged out of the water.

"Baby, I see two sharks," said Victoria.

"Yeah, you're right. I do, too," said Noah.

They observed the sharks feeding for nearly ten minutes. Despite being the season, the beach was empty that day, and few people noticed the activity. There was something about that image that situated deeply with Noah. It was a living-color example of survival-of-the-fittest. In many ways, it reminded him of Albert Abraham and CannaTron, a company that was built to survive at the expense of the employees' dreams. Noah knew that most of the remaining workers at CannaTron would stay with the company despite finding out about Albert's criminal activity and lies and being underpaid. Other than the educated like Bryan or even Zack, the rest had nowhere else to go, and Albert's broken promises of riches were all they had to look forward to.

The same didn't apply to Noah. He knew that Canna Tron would soon be just a memory. From the moment he was first hired,

Noah could sense the deviance and deception. He didn't put himself one hundred thousand dollars in debt with school loans to end up in a place like CannaTron. The time had come for him to find his next opportunity, one that rewarded his efforts and sacrifices up to that point in life.

"I think I'm going to quit," he said without hesitation.

"I knew that's where you were headed," said Victoria.

"CannaTron served its purpose. I would have never written or published that research paper if it wasn't for my time at the company. But for God's sake, they still don't offer sick days or vacation days. I thought I could handle that, but it's total bullshit. They say we're full-time employees, but we get treated like contractors. I need to find a real company to work for until I start my doctorate."

"So, is that it? Are you going back on Monday?"

"Yeah, I think so. I'll just start sending out my resume today, and hopefully, something good pops up before I quit," replied Noah.

They sat close to the water to gaze at the horizon. The sharks had moved on, leaving only the waves and the sky to admire. Victoria continued to look for seashells while Noah dug his feet in the sand. He laid his head on a mound and stared at the sky, taking a few deep breaths of air into his lungs.

"I'm so glad that we moved here. The beach is so close. We can come every day if we want," said Noah.

"We made a good decision to come here. The building has everything we need. The beach chairs, internet, and cable are included in the rent. I really think you should look for work that's closer to home. I don't want you making that drive anymore. It worries me," said Victoria.

"You're right, baby. I'm also happy that everything with the wedding has fallen into place," said Noah.

"Me too; I'm glad we've put down all the deposits. We can pay off the rest as we go," said Victoria after taking two hits. "I feel like the most stressful part is over."

"Me too, my love," replied Noah.

Along the shoreline, the Royal Terns aligned to absorb the remaining amount of sun for the day. Noah watched as they assembled like a military unit. The flock had two commanders, two trainers, and nine rookies. The commanders squawked orders at the rookies while the trainers flew overhead to display the instructions and test the dense winds. Once they returned to the flock, the little rookies took off and flew in a synchronized pattern against the wind.

Noah and Victoria walked back to the lounge chairs to gather their belongings and return home. Along the way, they were greeted by the splashing of another sea creature.

"You see that, baby?" said Noah.

"Whoa, is that another shark?" asked Victoria.

"No, that's a giant manta ray," replied Noah.

"A manta ray? I mean, I see that it's a different type of shadow. It's more like a black mass. But, how do you know?" asked Victoria.

"I used to fish off the Boynton inlet, which is up to the north about a quarter mile. I was enrolled in the work-study program during my senior year of high school. Technically, I worked for my parents, so I never really needed to show up. Instead, I would come straight from school at ten in the morning to fish with a cane pole. And that thing was always swimming up and down the inlet. The first time I saw it, I couldn't believe my eyes because it was so big. I saw it a few more times after that. I'm only assuming it's the same one because that thing out there is massive too. I'm surprised to see it again after more than fifteen years."

"Wow, this place is so amazing," said Victoria with peace in her eyes.

"I'm glad you're happy," said Noah before giving his future wife a kiss.

That beach, their open conversation, and their shared appreciation for peace, success, and pot was their formula for happiness. It was everything that Noah and Victoria needed to be happy together for the rest of their lives. With her, his life was perfect. In agreement with Kristin, Noah believed that CannaTron was a place full of negative energy. He never wanted that energy to overcome his judgment again.

Chapter 12
The Exit Sign

Noah returned to a quiet office on Monday. He walked around the cubicle area but didn't find anybody there, not Aziz. None of the sales girls, Bryan, Mitch, or Debbie, were in the office. He walked through the communal area and noticed that the coffee hadn't been made. It was usually the first sign that Elaine was there. He ventured to the front offices and didn't find David or Ian in the office they shared. Brittney's office door was closed as well.

The only noise that he heard came from Kenny's office. Noah walked by and saw the tortured CEO typing vigorously on the computer. He was wearing a t-shirt, shorts, and sandals and looked as though he hadn't slept for days. He looked like shit, barely functional, like his body was dead while his brain continued to work.

He was writing an e-mail to state officials in Oregon and Puerto Rico to explain a document that Jerry leaked about a deceptive act by CannaTron during a demo session for Oregon officials. Jerry hoped to sway Puerto Rico's decision about using CannaTron for their cannabis tracking program. He wrote about the way Albert and Kenny often recounted a story about the day they "pulled a fast one" over Oregon State officials en route to winning the state contract. Jerry said that they would recall the story to anyone who was willing to listen. The e-mail read:

...The deception occurred on the day that CannaTron presented the software to members of the Oregon Liquor Control Commission. On that day, Kenny Cho's CannaTron software from

his computer was unable to get a Wi-Fi signal while inside the presentation room. He was afraid that the system would appear to be inoperable or flawed. Instead of mentioning the misfortune to the state officials, he lied.

Kenny and Albert Abraham e-mailed AJ Lauria, who was offsite but not far. They told AJ to activate an inoperable mock-up program that he had created, which replicated essential functions in the CannaTron software. AJ later delivered the new computer, and Kenny deceived the state officials by presenting the software on a non-functioning platform. All he had to do was present the system on the big screen and explain the fields and functionality. All the while, the state officials thought they were viewing a finished, functioning product...

Jerry finished the e-mail letter by saying that Albert couldn't be trusted to conduct business in the cannabis industry. He said that Albert posed a threat to the industry, to local and state government agencies, and to employees and investors of CannaTron. The disgruntled lawyer ended the e-mail with:

...It is my professional and personal belief that any industry that Mr. Albert Abraham is involved in should be aware of his unethical and illegal actions. He is a fraud and sociopath in every sense of the word.

"Kenny, what's up? Where is everyone?" asked Noah.

"Um, nobody's here?" replied Kenny.

"No, how's Albert?"

"He's fine. It was a very mild heart attack. The hospital kept him for observation over the weekend, but he went home last night."

"Oh, that's excellent news. I was worried. I hadn't heard anything all weekend," lied Noah.

"Hey, uh, now that you're here, good work on the RFP. I know I haven't been around as much as I'd like, but it's good to know I can rely on you," said Kenny.

Noah was caught off guard by the comment. Based on Kenny's usual arrogance, his naturally lazy eyes, the constant exhaustion on his face, and the fact that he was a pothead, Noah always thought Kenny was giving him the stink eye. He thought that Kenny didn't like him. The compliment certainly wasn't expected, especially since he didn't use Noah's work for the final RFP. That was something that Noah, a writer, couldn't forget or forgive.

"So, why didn't you use my content?" he asked without hesitation.

Kenny froze from the fear of having to answer Noah. He was a small and skinny nerd, and Noah could tear him apart if he wanted. He also didn't want to admit that Noah was a better writer. Overall, he was intimidated by Noah for his physical advantages and intellectual capabilities.

"Noah, I... I felt that I needed to inject the proposal with more of my voice and less technical writing. You did an excellent job of providing me with clear, legible content that answered all the questions. But the final piece needed to have soul, and that's where I specialize," said Kenny. Noah was insulted and couldn't stop himself from firing back at Kenny.

"Well, I reviewed the RFP, and it came out like shit. I really wish that you had told me that all you wanted was data procurement. I could have edited your responses, and we would have had a better chance of winning. Your grammar was terrible, there were run-on sentences throughout, and the formatting was sloppy." Noah didn't stop there. He wanted to cleanse his mind before quitting. "And also, Zack's stupid statement was a result of your poor management. He should have never gone to Puerto Rico. You're the reason that we lost the RFP bid."

"I think the best thing we can do right now is to learn from this mistake and move forward, okay?" said Kenny to abruptly end the conversation. He knew Noah was right and gave him the respect he deserved for his bravery. He could have fired him, but he succumbed to his exhaustion and accepted the truth.

"Alright, sounds good," replied Noah before walking out of Kenny's office. He said what he had to say and got away with it. He thought he would get fired but was surprised that it didn't happen.

Kenny tried to proceed to work, but his focus had completely faded. He stood up and locked the door to his office. After returning to his desk, he took out a bottle of Adderall and frantically crushed one of the pills. He put his head down and snorted every spec that was on his desk. Then he jolted his head back as the bitter drip traveled down his pharynx. The pressure of being CEO became too much for Kenny to handle, leaving his mind in a twisted mess.

The rest of the employees eventually arrived to work that day. One by one, Noah saw them walk into the office as he finished his second blog of the morning. The last person to walk into the office that day was Bryan Miller. As usual, he whistled a jolly theme while still wearing his sunglasses.

"Mi amigo, como esta?" asked Bryan.

"What's up, my man? How are you?" replied Noah.

"I... am... excellent. Peep this homie, I just got these mailed to me from Washington," said Bryan while taking out a bag of mushrooms from his pocket.

"Oh, shit! How are they?" replied Noah.

"Smooth. It's not the strongest high, but there are definitely visuals if you eat enough. I took some last night, and today I woke up fresh."

"Are you selling any?" asked Noah. "Shit, I haven't done shrooms in a long time."

"No hay problemo. My buddy sent me more than I know what to do with. Take these. Just let me take some caps for my morning coffee," said Bryan. "And, uh, just a note. They don't fuck around in Washington. These things are potent. Have you heard anything about Albert?"

"Thanks, man. Um, yeah, he's alive. Kenny said it was a mild heart attack," replied Noah.

"More like Jerry scared him shitless," replied Bryan. "I'll be surprised if he ever shows his face here. I mean, I don't know what the fuck I'm going to do. But until I pass the Bar, this is as good as it gets for me."

"At least you have an office," said Noah sarcastically.

"Yeah, you're right about that. It's like my mom said, at any other company, I wouldn't be the Director of shit."

"So that's the official title? Director?" asked Noah.

"Bro, take advantage and choose the title that you want. Brodi has his job title as VP of Government Compliance on a co-worker. Brittney's profile says she is a Director of Government Proposals. And those two don't do shit. They never even went to school."

Noah was touched by Bryan's generosity. Although nobody could tell, he was once a fan of mushrooms during a more colorful stage of his youth. His life with Victoria changed his persona drastically. He was no longer the beer-swilling, street-fighting, shroom-tripping animal he used to be. Bryan's mushrooms would serve as a small reminder of a past that no longer existed.

Just as the day was ending, Brittney went around the office to inform all the employees that Kenny was having an emergency meeting about the alleged accusations against Albert and the company. Everybody gathered in the conference room just like they did during the stock meeting, but the mood wasn't the same. The ambiance was quiet as everybody waited for Kenny to arrive. They all wanted answers and to confirm the validity of Jerry's accusations.

Brittney entered the doors and walked to the front of the room to address everybody before the meeting. She wanted to prepare them for whatever would happen next. She'd spent the most time with Kenny and witnessed his mental decline more than anybody. Her concern was that Kenny was too unstable and unpredictable to give a presentation.

"Hey, guys. Thanks for coming. I know this is last minute, and we all want to go home. But there is something that needs to be addressed before you leave. Kenny will be here in a minute. By now, we're all aware of the attack that we're receiving from our former lawyer, Jerry Levine. Look, this is all a surprise to me. We all know Jerry and never expected him to turn on the company in this way. But the guy is going out of his way to lie about everybody and everything, about all of us, about you. Kenny is doing everything that he can to rectify this situation and stop Jerry from smearing our name."

Noah wouldn't allow her to speak any longer. *The audacity!* he thought. The tides had turned, and he finally had Brittney in a place where she was vulnerable. He didn't care any longer about getting fired. There was a matter of accountability to address because everyone there had been lied to.

"What is it?" she said unfavorably to Noah, who indicated that he wanted to speak.

"I follow Jerry's business page, and he never said anything about any of us. He's very clear as to who he's targeting. So, can you please just stick to the facts? I think we deserve that," said Noah.

"Are you really going to do this right now? I guess you don't feel like you're one of us," replied Brittney.

"That doesn't mean shit to me, Brittney. Albert is a fraud. Jerry's not lying. He's just exposing the truth. Everybody in this room was lied to," said Noah.

"And how do you know that those things he wrote were true?" replied Brittney with a snarky tone.

"Because he looked at me, at all of us in the eye, and lied! There's no fucking stock or employee incentive program. It's all bullshit!" yelled Noah.

Brittney was dumbfounded. She was unable to formulate a response because she knew that he was right. The others just stayed quiet. They were in disbelief at Noah's dominance over the situation. Seconds later, Kenny entered through the glass doors of the conference room after having heard the shouting between Noah and Brittney.

"We need to have a meeting with Noah about company loyalty," said Brittney with a broken tone and red eyes on the verge of tearing.

Kenny didn't want to dig into that matter. He only wanted to address the leaks and return to his office as quickly as possible. He held a melodic demeanor as the others expected him to regulate the situation. But that wouldn't happen because Kenny was already defeated.

"Noah, can you please sit down while I address everybody? This won't take long," said the CEO. Noah wanted to hear what the man had to say and sat down without any further comment. Brittney rushed to her office and closed the door to wipe away her tears in private.

"Team, thank you for meeting with me," said Kenny with bloodshot eyes. "First thing I want to inform all of you is that Albert is currently at home recovering from a mild heart attack. That's all that I was told. He's in good spirits and hopes to be back soon. He wants you to know that everything is fine."

Kenny walked across the room with his head down, trying to compose his thoughts. He rubbed his hands on his face to try and massage away some of the stress. After taking a deep breath, he continued.

"I'm also here to address the matter that we're facing against our former lawyer, Jerry Levine, whom you all know. I want to assure you that the board is in complete control of the situation. The information that Jerry claims as true is nothing but a lie in an attempt to extort this company for money."

"Fine, but what does that mean about our stock? What was that meeting all about?" asked Mitch.

"That meeting was exactly for what you were promised, a guaranteed percentage in company stock at the moment that we are bought and go public."

"According to Jerry, that's all crap. We weren't given an incentive. You just told us that without providing information that's needed to make such a determination," said Noah. "And according to Jerry, we were all played like a bunch of fools. I think we deserve to know the company's stock valuation right now."

The others saw Noah in a new light, one of leadership and fearlessness. They were thinking about what he was saying, but nobody wanted to risk their job. Noah had nothing left to offer the company and faced no consequences for speaking his mind.

"This is not the time nor place to discuss the company's valuation, Noah. I'm just here to reiterate that these are all lies. Albert is not a fraud. We are not a deceptive company. Those of you who have vested one year in the company owns a percentage of company stock. I need to make that clear. You are the heart and soul of this company. Without you, none of this is possible."

"What about the rumor that CymexGrow is interested in becoming the company's leading shareholder? I mean, is that our buy-off? That's what the incentive program states, correct?" asked Charlie as Brittney walked back into the room.

"There are multiple companies looking to invest in Canna Tron. This is what we have worked towards. Only with capital partners can we obtain the money necessary to take this company to the next level."

Nobody could believe what they were hearing. By that point, they all knew that Kenny was hiding information. Their leader couldn't cover the deceit anymore. It only confirmed the validity of Jerry's leaks.

"That still doesn't answer the question...," continued Charlie until Kenny interrupted him, exposing his dual-sided nature.

"I fucking told you there's no problem! Fuck! Fuck! Fuck!" yelled Kenny like a possessed madman before he pulled the intercom from the table and threw it at the presentation television. The screen shattered, and Kenny stormed out of the room to lock himself in his office. It was truly a remarkable sight to see for everybody in that room.

"I guess that's it," said Brittney before leaving for a second time.

The entire debacle left Noah in the mood to celebrate with the shrooms that Bryan gave him. He went home that evening and ate them while Victoria visited her parents in Kendall. Once he was alone, Noah ate a handful of capsules before 6 pm, giving him enough time to experience the high and get to bed before midnight.

For the first hour, Noah sat on his couch and watched the sports network, waiting to experience a visual. Instead, his body became relaxed and sunk deeper and deeper into the couch with every passing minute. His head started to feel light, and the sounds from the television became clearer than ever.

In the second hour, his vision became wavy. There were no strong visuals, but he could feel his body succumbing to the mushrooms. It wasn't until his first yawn that the tears started to drip from his eyes. Tearing was a secondary effect of the mushrooms and didn't stem from emotion. It was from the muscarine, a mushroom component that stimulated his muscarinic receptors in the parasympathetic nervous system. It was a sign that his eyes had dilated and a trip was imminent.

By the third hour, Noah could no longer focus on anything other than the trip. He saw strong, wave-like visuals. The city lights became piercing twinkles in his vision. The more he let his eyes and body relax, the stronger the visuals became. The yawning and tearing became uncontrollable. Noah no longer felt in control of his body. He fell to the side and stayed lying in that position for the rest of the night, moaning, groaning, and laughing simultaneously. It was the strongest trip that he'd ever experienced.

After reaching its peak, the high began to descend in waves. The numbing feeling became weaker, and then strong, and then weaker, and then strong again. Noah didn't want Victoria to come home and find him that way. So, he eventually got off the couch and walked to his bed. The effects continued to diminish for the rest of the evening, making it hard to fall asleep.

He woke up the next morning in a daze. After checking on Victoria, he stepped out of bed and walked to the bathroom. He had a bowel movement while recalling the strength of the mushrooms. As he washed his hands, Noah gave himself a look in the mirror. That was when he noticed his eyeball. The lateral side of his right cornea was red, as though a vessel had ruptured. He started to wonder if it was a result of the shrooms, from all the tearing that he experienced. Other than that, he felt as relaxed as he'd felt in a long time.

Noah sat at his desk and again noticed the silence. It was quieter than ever, leaving him to wonder if anyone would show up after seeing Kenny's meltdown. He was about to start writing something because there was never anything else to do until he froze and stared at the keyboard. There was an empty feeling in his gut, and he knew that his time there was finished. After realizing this, his phone vibrated, and he took it out of his pocket. It was Dr. Patel. Noah hoped that it was the call that he had been waiting for.

"Hello, Noah, good day. This is Dr. Patel."

"Dr. Patel, it's good to hear from you," replied Noah.

"Noah, I have great news. The editors at the journal have given your paper the final approval required for publication. It will be published next month. Congratulations," said Dr. Patel.

Noah pumped his hand in celebration while holding an intense look on his face. For the first time in his life, he knew the feeling of insuperable accomplishment. It felt like a small bolt of energy ascending from the pit of his gut to his throat. He took a deep breath to absorb the excitement but struggled to speak from the emotion he felt.

"Hello?" said Dr. Patel.

"I'm sorry. That's great news," replied Noah.

"I will send you the link as soon as it's available; good work, take care," said Dr. Patel.

Noah was overjoyed. He stepped out of the office and down the elevator to the first floor to bask in the glory. Never, not in a million years, did he think that one day he would be published in a medical journal, but it was fate all along. When nobody was around, he slipped behind a wall and clasped his hands together to give thanks to his creator.

He returned to the elevator and found the chief scientist, Alonzo Iverson, waiting in the lobby. Alonzo worked on the seventh floor, which Albert bought and renovated to hold his programming team. Other than a few run-ins, Noah had never said more than two words to Alonzo. He was too close of a talker for Noah's liking, making him feel uncomfortable during those brief interactions.

"Hi, Noah, good to see you," said the soft-spoken African American with light eyes.

"Hi, Alonzo, how are you?" cordially replied Noah.

"I'm good. It's a beautiful day, right?" said Alonzo while gently looking at Noah.

"Yup," replied Noah, who didn't care to make eye contact.

They stepped into the elevator, and Alonzo asked, "What floor?"

"I'm going back to the office, sixth floor," said Noah. "Thank you."

"Oh, okay, so, going up," said Alonzo. He pressed the number six button as the door closed.

"I love these things," continued Alonzo as Noah was staring at the door.

"Love what?" replied Noah.

"These elevators. You can go anywhere you want on them. You can go up. You can go down. You can do down on me in here," said Alonzo without any shame.

"What?" replied Noah, who couldn't believe what he'd just heard.

"You can go down on me if you want," replied Alonzo. Noah felt rage pierce through his head. He only had a split second to decide how to react. He was either going to berate, threaten, or frighten Alonzo for his audacity. Or, he was going to take the high road and walk away.

"Why the fuck are you even asking me that? No! I'm engaged to a beautiful woman! I can't believe this shit," expressed Noah as the elevator doors opened on the sixth floor. He took the high road and stepped out of the elevator with a disgusted look on his face.

He marched directly to Brittney's office to report the incident. Although he was ready to quit his job, Noah still thought that sexual harassment should always go on record. He was completely fed up with everything that CannaTron stood for and wasn't going to allow such an issue to remain undocumented.

"I need to talk to you," said Noah.

"Why? What's up? Close the door," replied Brittney, who sensed the urgency by the look on Noah's face.

"Yeah, uh, this is a little embarrassing," he said while taking a seat.

"God, what happened to your eye? It's bleeding," replied Brittney.

Noah looked at himself in a small mirror that Brittney had on her desk. His entire eye was blood red. The small spec that he noticed in the morning had covered his entire cornea.

"Oh, fuck. This has gotten worse," said Noah.

"Are you okay? Do you need to go to the hospital?" asked Brittney.

"Yeah, I'm fine. Um, but back to what happened. I just had the new chief scientist, Alonzo, hit on me in the elevator. He asked me to go down on him."

"What? Are you sure?" asked Brittney while also laughing a bit.

"Yes," said Noah, who became annoyed with her lack of sensitivity. "We stepped into the elevator. He asked me what floor. I told him the sixth floor. He said something about the elevator going up and down. And then he asked if I wanted to go down on him."

"What did you say?" asked Brittney.

"What? What do you mean? I told him no, and I got out of there."

"God, Noah, there's so much going on right now. I can't believe you're bringing this to me. I really don't need this at the moment," said Brittney with the most insincere look on her face.

"Are you fucking kidding me? I tell you that I was sexually harassed by another employee, and that's how you respond. Fuck you, Brittney! And fuck this place," said Noah before leaving her office.

Brittney chased Noah down to his cubicle, where he was

gathering his belongings.

"Don't talk to me like that and walk out of my office. Who do you think you are!?" she yelled.

"I'm somebody who doesn't need this bullshit. You have no other choices in life because you have no education, and nobody loves you. You're mean and intolerable. I quit," said the hot-tempered Latino.

"What? You can't quit. Come back, Noah!" pleaded Brittney.

But there was nothing left to say. Noah had had enough of CannaTron, and it was time for him to go. His paper was published, and he had no more reason to stay there. For the foreseeable future, his time in the cannabis industry was over.

Chapter 13
All That's Meant to Happen

Jerry Levine continued his mission to destroy the company. For months after Noah's departure, he posted and reposted content that rattled the industry. Eventually, Jerry even started to attack Sam Williams on the internet, letting everyone know how he was threatened by an executive member of the Florida Bar Association. In return, Sam Williams used his power and got the Florida Bar Association to file a complaint against Jerry for slander. He used screenshots of Jerry's social media posts as evidence. And, of course, Jerry made it known to his social media following that he was being attacked by "Babylon," as he called it, and its "Bumbaclots."

He claimed to be a "white lion en route to Zion" while being interviewed on a cannabis business radio show called "Wake n Bake with Donna Summers." The show was hosted by a pretentious hippie from Trinidad, Colorado, whose smoke lounge had recently been raided and shut down by federal agents. She connected with Jerry on the social media site, CoWorker and invited him to call into the show to discuss her case and the legal barriers for business owners in the industry.

"I'd like to introduce Jerry Levine, the esquire. He's a nationally known cannabis lawyer from South Florida who also spends a lot of his time in Jamaica. He's a friend to Jamaica, a friend to the cannabis industry, and a friend to the show. Jerry, welcome!" said Donna Summers.

"Thank you, Donna. Thanks for having me on the show. I'm

actually in Jamaica right now for the High Times Awards," said Jerry.

"I am so jealous. I hope you have a wonderful time."

"It's always a wonderful time here," replied Jerry.

"Wonderful, so, to begin, can you please tell us a bit about your history in the cannabis industry?" asked Donna.

"Sure, well, my history in the cannabis industry started a long time ago when I was a law student at NYU. I was a writer for the NYU Law Review and published a few articles that questioned the classification of cannabis as a schedule one drug. At the time, the only law that existed with regard to cannabis were criminal laws. I worked in securities and transactions on the business side, but I never worked in criminal law. Therefore, because of my business background, I bring a different perspective to what's going on in the cannabis industry."

"So, I mentioned my case earlier in the show to the audience. Can you tell us what you think are the biggest hurdles that a cannabis consumption business has? There are multiple clubs like mine that simply want to enjoy a relaxing environment with quality conversation while enjoying cannabis. Why are federal regulators teaming with local officials to shut down these businesses? It's simply a social club," said Donna.

"Exactly, that's what it is, a social club. I think it's a great idea. People enjoy a place where they can socialize with like-minds, and that's what the cannabis lounge presents," said Jerry.

"But how can they be regulated? How can the state make money off these social clubs if there is no money transaction occurring? It's a place where people bring their cannabis. None of it is sold at the lounges. So, my question is, why is there a need for regulations?" asked Donna.

"Again, I think it would be great to have a social club where I could meet peaceful individuals while enjoying my own cannabis at my own leisure. The issue with overseeing agencies is the safety measures and the potential for illegal activity occurring. But there are ways to maintain your business while still complying with state laws. You either have to charge a membership fee or align yourself with a dispensary that sells cannabis. I'd compare it to a cigar-smoking lounge where one can purchase a stogie and enjoy it in the lounge area. California is one place where social clubs like this exist. But there, it involves a membership fee and an overall corporate element to it," advised Jerry.

"That's interesting. It's never been presented to me in such a clear way. But why not repeal cannabis prohibition and enjoy the proceeds that follow?" asked Donna.

"That's the million-dollar question. It really comes down to the federal level. This new head of the DOJ hopes to come down hard on the industry, and the likelihood of the Cole-memo being reversed is actually possible. To counter that, it's really important that cannabis businesses are fully compliant and aren't conducting deceitful business practices. Remember, if Congress wanted to, they could also repeal cannabis prohibition tomorrow in a half hour. It wouldn't take them long to make it legal and subject to the Controlled Substance Act for schedule one drugs."

"So, what's the problem? Is there too much money involved? Are there too many stigmas and regulatory costs to get this thing repealed?"

"You nailed it," replied Jerry.

"So, what's one message that you want to give out to the industry? There are a lot of small business owners invested in this industry and a lot of potential investors too. More than seven billion dollars rolled through the state of Colorado alone last year. What's your opinion of these entrepreneurs?" continued Donna.

"Cannabis is an affordable source of alternative energy that's ready to be utilized, in addition to the medical benefits. The industry is there, ready to fly. Run a compliant, innovative business with strong financial backing. Build a winning business model where finances are in line with investments, costs, and gains. This helps to minimize uncertainty and loss of capital," replied Jerry.

"Thank you for that, Jerry. Your time here has certainly been helpful to our listeners," said Donna.

"You're welcome. I just want to add one more thing. I stress the need for ethical business practices because there are currently companies at the top of our little food chain who refuse to accept responsibility for their deceitful ways. I won't name names, but certain players down in Florida have no business in this industry and are only ruining it for the rest of us."

"What do you mean by deceitful ways?" asked Donna.

"I mean purposefully lying to government officials, sexual harassment accusations, ties to illegal criminal activities. Guys who run businesses like this only paint a poor picture of how good this industry can actually be. As a white lion on Jah's mission, I make it my business to call out Babylon and hold them accountable for the atrocities that they have committed against so many people."

CannaTron tried to continue moving forward with daily

operations despite losing more than five hundred customers in three months. But the reality of it all was that the product was still unique for the growing industry. E-Greens' popularity was rising, but CannaTron's patented Application Program Interface was the core competence that government officials needed to properly track the production cycle and sale of cannabis.

The solution was so unique that CymexGrow eventually purchased all of Albert's and Frank Delfino's shares in CannaTron for an undisclosed amount. As predicted, Albert and Delfino dumped their stock, making CymexGrow the single largest shareholder in the company. It was Albert's largest payday and his official exit from the company and its mayhem. As a serial entrepreneur, he'd accomplished what he'd always set out to do.

CymexGrow put their CEO, Michael Cavanaugh, on CannaTron's board of directors. He didn't waste time initiating executive orders and tearing up the infrastructure. In the end, all CymexGrow wanted was the product. They didn't give two shits about the company, its employees, or any bullshit promise of stock. For the workers of CannaTron, everything proved to be nothing more than a pump-and-dump scam. They were promised riches, but ultimately, their shares were worth a fraction of a penny. The ones who stayed were offered a severance package of two months before being fired.

The dismissals started with Jamie and Kristin. Cavanaugh appointed Brittney the dirty deed of firing her old friends. To make things stranger, they were each called into Brittney's office by fellow Ratchet Crew member Ian. Kristin took the news well. She hardly reacted when Brittney told her that she was being released. She accepted her check, got her bag and keys, and left the building. Kristin eventually moved to Colorado and lived her life in a community of hippies, teaching daily meditation classes for free and getting drunk every night.

Jamie didn't leave without a rant. She cursed out Brittney. She cursed out Ian. She ripped the earnings board from the wall. And she threw her computer off her desk. Ultimately, Jamie ended up where she started. After realizing that she was a full-blown lesbian during a drunken binge, she returned to work at a strip club in North Miami where men grabbed her ass daily.

Mitch went down like a captain in a sinking ship. He hoped that his loyalty would pay off, but it never did. Michael Cavanaugh gave him his severance, and he reacted by sharing his idea on another branding campaign. He showed up to work for an additional two days until the police were called to take him away.

Debbie stayed around until a licensed CPA was hired to oversee the company's finances. She stayed long enough to assist him in procuring old financial statements and tax forms. Like Mitch, she thought that she had a chance to stay. Her efforts were a final attempt to keep her job and prove that she was useful. But it was all for nothing. She walked into her office one morning and found all her things in boxes. The new CPA was sitting at her desk and told her that she was no longer needed.

"At least you get to keep the notepads," he said as she unfavorably carried her things out of the office.

After Albert's departure, Ian was kept around to help Michael Cavanaugh transition into his new role. It was heartbreaking for him to work for anyone other than Albert, especially for someone who was straight with a wife and kids. It was just as hard for Michael to accept Ian's flamboyant and feminine personality. He was a conservative Republican. After only one month, Ian quit and opted to become Albert's house-boy at the mansion on a full-time basis.

Aziz accepted his severance and left quietly. He was the only one who never fully depended on CannaTron's success. Although he worked tireless hours and was distraught over the company stock, he was still a licensed pharmacist. He eventually opened another pharmacy and returned to selling prescription pain pills on the black market.

Kenny and Brittney were the last to go. They stayed working as a tandem, with their heads down, ignoring the others who left and being ignored by the new workers who arrived. Brittney tried to maintain her status, but nobody listened to her. Eventually, she became riddled with anxiety. It wasn't until she tried to reprimand a new employee that she realized how insignificant she became at the company.

The new project manager, a hotshot shark, was often late by a few minutes because of her long commute, much like Noah. Brittney, trying to remain the alpha- female, decided to schedule a meeting to discuss the tardiness. The project manager walked into the office to find Brittney at her desk with her usual bitch-face.

"Hi, Laura. Thanks for meeting with me," said Brittney as she took off her reading glasses. "Look, this is going to be quick. I notice that you come in every day at 9:06, and I can't have that. You need to start getting here before or at 9 am; otherwise, I'll have to write you up."

Laura sat in the chair across from Brittney and started to smile before giggling. It surely wasn't the response that Brittney expected.

"Why are you laughing?" she asked.

"Because I know about you. You and that other guy, Kenny, the one who never leaves his office," said Laura. "You mean the CEO?" replied Brittney.

"Yeah, whatever; you two are some of the last ones here," said Laura as Brittney struggled to accept the reality of the situation. "What? Haven't you noticed? Well, when you do, go fetch me some coffee 'cause you're just a secretary, bitch."

Laura stood up and left Brittney at a loss for words. She only returned two minutes later to deliver a message from the new boss. "Hey, Michael and I just had a meeting. He wants to see you in his office."

Brittney walked to Michael's office, formerly Albert's office. She was nervous and frightened. The room was no longer decorated in lavish, antique furniture. He removed the carpet, added tile, and went for a colder look. He was on a mission to transform that company and turn a profit and didn't care for aesthetics.

"Hi, Michael. You called for me?" said Brittney with a concerned look on her face.

"Hi, Brittney, yes, uh, I need my car washed and my laundry picked up," said Michael before throwing Brittney his keys.

"I thought you wanted me to schedule the board meeting," replied Brittney.

"It's not necessary anymore," said Michael while looking at his computer.

For Brittney, it was an unbearable realization that she wouldn't become a millionaire overnight. In her mind, she earned the big payoff and struggled to accept that Kenny wasn't going to fix the situation and find a way for them to keep their stock.

Two hours later, she returned to the office with lunch and laundry in hand and walked directly to Mr. Cavanaugh's office to return the keys. She found him on the phone and opted to leave his clothes hanging on a coat rack. She left his keys on his desk and tried to walk out quietly until Mr. Cavanaugh said, "Brittney, don't go far." She sat down and waited for five minutes until he was finished with the phone call. As soon as he hung up the phone, he let Brittney know her fate.

"Brittney, this was your last task at CannaTron. I thank you for your service and commitment, but Elaine has been promoted to your position. Please, leave your keycard with me and gather your belongings. Elaine will escort you out," said Michael as Elaine walked into the room. Suddenly, Brittney felt a rolling ball of anxiety move through her gut. She couldn't believe what was happening.

Elaine filed her nails in blissful redemption as she watched Brittney box her belongings. While walking out of the office, she lost her footing and dropped her box, sending multiple items across the floor. Elaine didn't flinch to help. She just stood there watching in glee while swinging her keycard in circles in the air. Brittney was on her knees when she noticed Elaine tapping her foot as though she had better things to do.

"Lucky for me that Michael and I dated in high school," flaunted Elaine. Brittney was experiencing an utter reversal of fortune, a true example of karma.

Brittney grabbed all her items and put them into the same box.

She didn't look at Elaine once in the eyes as she left her office for the last time. They arrived at the waiting room, where Elaine opened the door. Brittney walked out of the office, but not without receiving a proper goodbye from Elaine.

"Good riddance, bitch," she said before slamming the door.

Kenny's departure from the company was a gradual process. At first, Michael Cavanaugh had him thinking that they were going to be Co-CEOs, running and directing the future path of the company as a team. But after a month, it became apparent that there was only one boss. Michael simply picked his brain for all the information that he needed. After a few months, Kenny's workload diminished drastically. He was no longer involved in the RFP process, and he no longer spoke at board meetings. Eventually, he stopped being invited to them. All new business was being conducted by Michael Cavanaugh and his colleagues at CymexGrow. At the end of his tenure, Kenny was only being used as an industry consultant for Michael and as a scapegoat for the Jerry Levine lawsuit.

To make matters worse, Kenny eventually became the primary target of Jerry's online attacks. It irked the lawyer that the young CEO was willing to do anything to protect Albert from going to jail. The company continued to re-schedule deposition dates, which caused Jerry to file an emergency motion for a Protective Order for the costs incurred of filing the motion and other court fees. Jerry claimed that Kenny and Sam Williams were playing scheduling games and violating court orders. In retaliation, he posted memes that suggested that Kenny was Albert's stooge. The posts accused Kenny of honoring a protected felon while engaging in unethical business practices.

The declarations and accusations eventually caught the attention of Kenny's wife, Angela Cho. To her, CannaTron wasn't worth the trouble, and she wanted her husband to leave. But to Kenny, his position as CEO was all that he wanted to preserve, no matter the cost.

Kenny hadn't been home for two days, claiming he was working on a new RFP. Other than a few phone calls, he'd barely communicated with his wife. As a result, Angela's instincts pushed her to go and find him. Kenny always left a work keycard copy on his desk at home. So, she took that copy and used it to open the doors of the building and the office.

The lights were off, and the office doors were locked, all except Kenny's office, which was opened a crack. There was light seeping through that crack and a thumping noise coming out of the office. She pushed the door forward with her hand and found her husband naked and bent over his desk while being plowed by another man.

"What the fuck?" was all that she could say.

Kenny was terrified to hear her voice. He turned his head around and saw his wife standing there in shock. He was paralyzed by the fear. But nothing needed to be said. She just looked to the floor, turned around, and left the office.

"Angela! Angela! Please come back!" yelled Kenny as he ran naked to the elevators. But Angela was gone, and their marriage was over. She went home, packed her items and the dogs, and left Kenny. It was the last time that they would ever see each other. Noah's presumption turned out to be the truth.

Eventually, Jerry got word of the separation and used that as ammo against Kenny. He didn't know why the separation occurred;

nobody did. But he knew that it gave him a mental advantage over his adversary. Jerry posted images of Golden Retrievers and wrote captions such as, "We don't miss you, Daddy! We love Mommy's new guy! He's a real man."

He also posted pictures of Kenny and wrote, "Look who won't be feeling the love this Valentine's Day? His loving bride left him. She took the dogs and went to find another stud." The images crippled Kenny's soul. They rattled his existence, putting him on the verge of becoming severely ill.

One day, about three weeks after Angela left, Kenny drove his car to an extravagant mansion on the intra- coastal waterway. He drove up the massive driveway and parked the car next to the central fountain. He stepped out of his car and walked to the oak double doors at the house entrance. There was loud electronic dance music playing from inside the house as if a party was being thrown. Kenny rang the doorbell and stepped back onto the driveway.

To his surprise, Ian answered the door, shirtless and dancing like the almighty queen that he was. He was wearing colorful shades and was high on Molly. But overall, he looked happy.

"Oh my God, saucy! It's so good to see you," said Ian while continuing to move to the beat of the music that was playing throughout the house.

"How can I help you?" said Ian.

Then Albert came to the door in a Brunello Cucinelli bathrobe while holding a Scotch Whiskey in his left hand and a cigar in the other. He immediately noticed that Kenny was in disarray, in tears and tremoring.

"Kenny, are you alright? Would you like to come in?" asked Albert.

Without warning, Kenny pulled out a nine-millimeter handgun and put it in his mouth. He looked Albert in the eyes and took two deep breaths. Albert tried to say something, but before any words came out, Kenny pulled the trigger and blew his brains on Albert's front porch. His body collapsed, and blood poured out of his head and down the entranceway.

Zack Stansbury was denied his shares through a court order, but AJ paid him back for the loan plus the interest. After CannaTron, he floated through life as a loan shark until he eventually tried to open his own cannabis consulting business in California. He found an investor to fund his first year of operations. But as always, Zack linked himself to a thug, a delinquent. When he was unable to pay back his return, the capitalist hired muscle to break Zack's legs and beat him to within an inch of his life.

Although the company was under new management and none of the former employees received their stock incentives, Jerry remained at war with CannaTron. His obsession wouldn't allow him to quit his assault on the company, not until he got paid, no matter who was in charge. He knew what he was owed, and he knew how to fight it. Therefore, he didn't hesitate to heckle CannaTron and its new investors on the internet. Jerry cast them as thieves and fools who invested in a failing product. All in all, Jerry was at war with Albert, Canna Tron's investors, CannaTron's former executive board, the Florida Bar Association, and Sam Williams. His witch hunt led him to make enemies with powerful people who wanted him dead.

Jerry couldn't care less. In his mind, he was a tough New

Yorker who didn't get intimidated by thugs. One night, he was trolling the internet while smoking some White Widow from a bong. He was in the middle of editing another image of Kenny and his dogs when an unknown assailant broke into the house and pointed a gun at the back of his head.

"Don't you fucking turn around. I'm going to stand here until you delete all of your social media accounts. If you move in any way, I'll fucking kill you," said the assailant in a muffled tone. "Do you understand?"

"Hey, no problem, no problem. You see. I'm getting rid of all of it. Just don't kill me," pleaded Jerry while tampering with the computer.

The assailant waited for five minutes as Jerry deactivated his accounts, one by one. The lawyer never turned around the entire time. He was only able to see a reflection of the assailant in the window but couldn't identify the person. His only focus was to cooperate and stay alive as long as possible. But unfortunately for him, the hit had already been paid for.

"Okay, that's all of them," said Jerry.

Without warning, the assailant pulled the trigger and shot Jerry in the back of the head at close range. His head split in two, and his torso flew forward, sending brain remnants on the wall and on the table. The carcass slammed onto the table, and blood spewed to the floor. Jerry was left to rot for five days until his ex-wife reported him missing to the police. The killer was never identified.

Eight Months Later...

It was the holiday season. Noah and Victoria were shopping in a busy outlet center in West Palm Beach. They were accompanied by a cool breeze, a clear evening sky, and the twinkling stars of the south. That night, Noah and Victoria were walking a little lighter than usual. They'd finally received the news that they were waiting for, and Noah couldn't stop reading the e-mail on his phone. It was his letter of acceptance from the University of Miami School of Medicine.

"I can't believe that I've finally been accepted to a Ph.D. program. Did you ever think we would get here?" said Noah.

"I knew we would, eventually. I know you have that drive, but you stress yourself too much. I also think the wedding put us both over the edge at times," said Victoria.

They were strolling in a daze when Noah noticed somebody in the distance. The individual and a lady were walking together his way. As they approached each other, Noah realized that it was his former co-worker at CannaTron, Bryan Miller. He was also holiday shopping with his wife and celebrating as well.

"Mr. Miller! What's up, my man?" said Noah.

"There he is. What's up, Noah?" replied Bryan before the two embraced in a hug.

"Just soaking in some good news. I finally got accepted to the UM doctorate program," said Noah.

"Whoa, that's excellent. I knew it would happen," said Bryan before giving Noah a bro hug. "I also got some good news for you. I finally passed the bar exam."

"Whoa. This is awesome. Finally, a lawyer I can trust," said Noah. "Congratulations, my friend. Are you still at CannaTron?"

"No way. After everything that happened, I couldn't stay there. But I just got a job with E-Greens as an associate counsel. We're moving to Colorado in a month," said Bryan.

"There's no better place for you. Congratulations, homie," said Noah.

Noah was as happy for Bryan as he was for himself. The former co-workers spoke for a moment. But as always happens with co-workers, they lost touch, and it was the last time they would ever see each other. He and Victoria finished their rounds of shopping and walked to the car in the parking lot. Along the way, he held her close in his arms, looked at the sky, and thanked the heavens for his blessings.

THE END

About the Author

Fabian Hernandez is an American author. The son of immigrants, he was born in Louisiana and grew up in South Florida. He's earned a Bachelor's degree in Humanities and a Master's degree in Biomedical Sciences. Fabian combines his imagination, his attention to detail, and his love for the English language to create unique and compelling stories.